Supporting Children with Behaviour Issues in the Classroom

This completely revised edition is an easy to use resource for teachers, TAs and SEN-COs concerned about behavioural issues in the classroom. It will support school staff in their approach to a range of behavioural issues, through a range of tried-and-tested strategies, including:

- How to create an environment of support and acceptance
- Techniques to provide an effective learning environment
- Ways to communicate clearly with children with poor communication skills
- Whole class and whole-school approaches for a positive learning environment
- How to maintain appropriate behaviours during unstructured break times

This accessible reference tool will help any teacher to create and maintain a classroom environment conducive to learning. Packed with resources, it also includes templates and example Personal Support Plans, written by practitioners for practitioners.

Sarah Carr – Well-being Officer, Eastfield Primary School, Hull, UK.

Susan Coulter – Special School Headteacher, UK.

Elizabeth Morling – Series Editor, SEN Consultant and former Head of the Education Service for Physical Disability, Hull City Council, UK.

Rebecca Smith – Well-being Officer, Eastfield Primary School, Hull, UK.

nasen is a professional membership association that supports all those who work with or care for children and young people with special and additional educational needs. Members include teachers, teaching assistants, support workers, other educationalists, students and parents.

nasen supports its members through policy documents, journals, its magazine *Special*, publications, professional development courses, regional networks and newsletters. Its website contains more current information such as responses to government consultations. **nasen's** published documents are held in very high regard both in the UK and internationally.

Other titles published in association with the National Association for Special Educational Needs (nasen):

Assessing Children with Specific Learning Difficulties: A teacher's practical guide
Gavin Reid, Gad Elbeheri and John Everatt
2016/pb: 978-0-415-67027-2

Supporting Children with Down's Syndrome, 2ed
Lisa Bentley, Ruth Dance, Elizabeth Morling, Susan Miller and Susan Wong
2016/pb: 978-1-138-91485-8

Provision Mapping and the SEND Code of Practice: Making it work in primary, secondary and special schools, 2ed
Anne Massey
2016/pb: 978-1-138-90707-2

Supporting Children with Medical Conditions, 2ed
Susan Coulter, Lesley Kynman, Elizabeth Morling, Francesca Murray, Jill Wing and Rob Grayson
2016/pb: 978-1-138-91491-9

Achieving Outstanding Classroom Support in Your Secondary School: Tried and tested strategies for teachers and SENCOs
Jill Morgan, Cheryl Jones and Sioned Booth-Coates
2016/pb: 978-1-138-83373-9

Supporting Children with Sensory Impairment
Gill Blairmires, Cath Coupland, Tracey Galbraith, Elizabeth Morling, Jon Parker,

Annette Parr, Fiona Simpson and Paul Thornton
2016/pb: 978-1-138-91919-8

The SENCO Survial Guide, 2ed
Sylvia Edwards
2016/pb: 978-1-138-93126-8

Dyslexia and Early Childhood
Barbara Pavey
2016/pb: 978-0-415-73652-7

Supporting Children with Dyslexia, 2ed
Hilary Bohl and Sue Hoult
2016/pb: 978-1-138-18561-6

More Trouble with Maths: A teacher's complete guide to identifying and diagnosing mathematical difficulties, 2ed
Steve Chinn
2016/pb: 978-1-138-18750-4

Supporting Children with Cerebral Palsy, 2ed
Rob Grayson, Jillian Wing, Hannah Tusiine, Graeme Oxtoby and Elizabeth Morling
2017/pb: 978-1-138-18742-9

Supporting Children with Behaviour Issues in the Classroom, 2ed
Sarah Carr, Susan Coulter, Elizabeth Morling and Hannah Smith
2017/pb: 978-1-138-67385-4

Supporting Children with Behaviour Issues in the Classroom

Second Edition

Sarah Carr, Susan Coulter, Elizabeth Morling and Rebecca Smith

Routledge
Taylor & Francis Group
LONDON AND NEW YORK

Helping Everyone Achieve

This edition published 2017
by Routledge
2 Park Square, Milton Park, Abingdon, Oxon OX14 4RN

and by Routledge
711 Third Avenue, New York, NY 10017

*Routledge is an imprint of the Taylor & Francis Group,
an informa business*

First published in 2005 by David Fulton

British Library Cataloguing in Publication Data
A catalogue record for this book is available from the British Library

Library of Congress Cataloging in Publication Data
Names: Carr, Sarah, 1966-
Title: Supporting children with behaviour issues in the classroom /
Sarah Carr, Susan Coulter, Elizabeth Morling, Rebecca Smith.
Description: 2nd Edition. | New York : Routledge, 2017.
Identifiers: LCCN 2016007404 | ISBN 9781138673830 (Hardback :
alk. paper) | ISBN 9781138673854 (Paperback : alk. paper) | ISBN
9781315561653 (eBook)
Subjects: LCSH: Problem children–Education–Great Britain. |
Behavior disorders in children. | Special education–Great Britain.
Classification: LCC LC4801 .C3497 2017 | DDC 371.93–dc23LC
record available at https://lccn.loc.gov/2016007404

ISBN: 978-1-138-67383-0 (hbk)
ISBN: 978-1-138-67385-4 (pbk)
ISBN: 978-1-315-56165-3 (ebk)

Typeset in Helvetica
by Cenveo Publisher Services

Contents

SECTION 8
Continuing Professional Development   **95**

Foreword

This book was initially written by Anny Bibby, Mary Davey, Dee Hudson-Vaux, Susan Miller, Elizabeth Morling and Carol Stitt.

It has been rewritten to encompass new government legislation and current practices in education by:

Sarah Carr Wellbeing Officer, Eastfield Primary School
Rebecca Smith Wellbeing Officer, Eastfield Primary School
Susan Coulter: former Special School Headteacher
Elizabeth Morling, formerly Head of Service, Education Service for Physical Disability

With thanks to:

Dr Linda Evans
Berni Moorcroft, Tweendykes School, Hull
Rachel Davies, Oakfield School, Hull

The contributions from Collingwood Primary School, Eastfield Primary School and Withernsea Primary Academy are greatly appreciated.

Introduction

This book is written under the premise that good behaviour management is a requirement for effective teaching and learning: this is the case for **all** children, but especially for those who have a barrier to learning. Accordingly, the authors address general behaviour management and suggest strategies for creating and sustaining a classroom environment that is conducive to learning.

In addition, it is recognised that some children with ADD/ADHD, Down's syndrome, autism, those in socially disadvantaged situations and an increasing number who experience mental health problems will have particular issues with conforming to behaviour 'norms'.

A child who is in distress, who is making wrong choices and who is displaying anti-social behaviours is a child who is unable to cope with their current or past life experiences. Unwanted or inappropriate behaviour is a form of communication: the child or adolescent is communicating to the people around him that all is not well with his life. Teachers and teaching assistants who understand the organic and environmental issues that are impacting on a child's behaviour will be well placed to support that child successfully without *detriment to the rest of the class*. The table below lists a range of factors that may impact on a child's social, mental and emotional wellbeing.

Environmental issues may include	Organic issues may include
Chaotic home life, e.g. • Breakdown of parents' relationships • Breakdown of child/parent relationship • Parenting skills • Poverty; debt; drugs; alcohol abuse Self-esteem issues, e.g. • Bullying or bullied • Self perception/self worth • Self harm • Eating disorders	Immaturity Prematurity Nutritional issues – dietary/malabsorption Medical conditions and conduct disorders 　Attention deficit disorder 　Attention deficit hyperactive disorder (ADHD) 　Attachment disorder 　Autism 　Anxiety 　Developmental delay 　Depression 　Disruptive disorder 　Hearing loss 　Oppositional Defiance Disorder 　Pathological Demand Avoidance 　Schizophrenia or bipolar disorder

So… this book will cover both generic and specific approaches to managing children's behaviour, albeit in a concise fashion. Further reading and resources will be referenced for more in-depth information.

From time to time some children present behaviour that can be difficult to manage in a mainstream setting. However, factors such as the child's age, the context in which the behaviours are displayed, its frequency and other external factors can alter whether a child's behaviour is viewed as a typical part of growing up or a cause for concern. We passionately believe that in the majority of children, undesirable behaviour is in response to underlying causes outside their control. We emphasise the importance of separating the child or young person from the behaviour exhibited and looking at underlying causes. The authors stress the need for all those involved with a child who is demonstrating inappropriate behaviour to understand the child or young person. It could be that their home life is presenting challenges that they are struggling to deal with and that they need support to develop the resilience to overcome these challenges.

Emotional and social difficulties is a broad term, which is widely used within education. Within the Special Educational Needs and Disability Code of Practice, 2014 the term 'behaviour' is no longer used and is no longer identified as a primary special need. The focus is now on the underlying factors that are triggering inappropriate behaviours and are detrimental to pupils' development – emotional, social and academic.

Schools must provide a safe caring environment where every pupil is nurtured. This book acknowledges that there are many different approaches to supporting pupils with emotional and social difficulties: schools may choose one particular approach or a mixture tailored to suit the needs of their pupils. We offer staff a toolbox of tried and tested approaches, all with the intention of improving the wellbeing of pupils. Practitioners can take the parts they feel useful and perhaps explore some areas in greater detail, e.g. Restorative Practices, through further research. The book can be read as a whole or dipped into as necessary; there are overlaps within the book where identified areas have similar approaches to supporting pupils.

The table below illustrates the provision made by successful schools for the wellbeing of all children. Later sections will suggest approaches gathered by observing good and outstanding practice in a range of mainstream and special school settings.

A SAFE LEARNING ENVIRONMENT where Learning to learn skills are taught and valued Expectations and boundaries are consistent and fair Child's voice is heard and acted on	**CLEARLY ARTICULATED VALUES & ETHOS** where Policy is put into practice Approaches are agreed and consistent Rewards and sanctions are consistent and fair Staff actively try to catch children being good
POSITIVE RELATIONSHIPS THROUGH SHARED VISION Adult to adults – staff/staff; staff/parent Child to child Adult to child/child to adult	**ENGAGING CURRICULUM** Relevant to learners Both knowledge and skill based Experiential

A child in distress needs all of these plus a personalised approach based on knowledge from parents as experts about their child and the team around the child

Section 1

Legislation and guidance

1 Legislation and DfE guidance

The Special Educational Needs and Disability Code of Practice, 2014 states that:

Special educational needs and provision can be considered as falling under four broad areas.

1 Communication and interaction
2 Cognition and learning
3 Social, mental and emotional health
4 Sensory and/or physical

Many children and young people have difficulties that fit clearly into one of these areas; some have needs that span two or more areas.

(DfE 2014)

Social, mental and emotional health

Children and young people may experience a wide range of social, mental and emotional difficulties, which manifest themselves in many different ways:

- becoming withdrawn or isolated;
- displaying challenging, disruptive or disturbing behaviour.

These behaviours may reflect underlying mental health difficulties such as anxiety or depression, self-harming, substance misuse, eating disorders or physical symptoms that are medically unexplained. Other pupils may have disorders such as attention deficit disorder (ADD), attention deficit hyperactive disorder (ADHD) or attachment disorder.

A question of SEN

- Persistent disruptive or withdrawn behaviours do not necessarily mean that a child or young person has SEN.
- Where there are concerns, there should be an assessment to determine whether there are any causal factors such as undiagnosed learning difficulties, difficulties with communication or mental health issues.
- Other events can lead to learning difficulties or wider mental health difficulties, such as bullying or bereavement. Such events will not always lead to children

having SEN but can have an impact on wellbeing and sometimes this can be severe. Schools should ensure they make appropriate provision for a child's short-term needs in order to prevent problems escalating. Where there are long-lasting difficulties schools should consider whether the child might have SEN.

Special educational needs (SEN)

Persistent mental health difficulties may cause pupils to have significantly greater difficulty in learning and it may be necessary to identify the pupil as having a special educational need.

The Special Educational Needs and Disability Code of Practice, 2014 states:

A child or young person has SEN if they have a learning difficulty or disability which calls for special educational provision to be made for him or her. A child of compulsory school age or a young person has a learning difficulty or disability if he or she:

- has a significantly greater difficulty in learning than the majority of others of the same age, or
- has a disability which prevents or hinders him or her from making use of educational facilities of a kind generally provided for others of the same age in mainstream schools or mainstream post-16 institutions.

In addition:

All children and young people are entitled to an education that enables them to:

- achieve their best;
- become confident individuals living fulfilling lives; and
- make a successful transition into adulthood, whether into employment, further or higher education or training.

The Teachers Standards (Department of Education 2012) further strengthens the Code of Practice, 2014 guidance that states that every teacher must make provision for **all** children.

A teacher must:

Set goals that stretch and challenge pupils of all backgrounds, abilities and dispositions
Adapt teaching to respond to the strengths and needs of all pupils ... and be able to use and evaluate distinctive teaching approaches to engage and support them.

Advice from the Department for Education

All pupils will benefit from learning and developing in a well ordered school environment that fosters and rewards good behaviour and sanctions poor and disruptive behaviour. Our *behaviour and discipline in schools* advice sets out the powers

8

and duties for school staff and approaches they can adopt to manage behaviour in their schools.

(Mental Health and Behaviour in Schools, 2016)

It also says that schools should consider whether continuing disruptive behaviour might be a result of unmet educational or other needs.

2 Discipline in schools – teachers' powers and the use of reasonable force

Sections 90 and 91 of the Education and Inspections Act 2006 gives teachers:

- statutory authority to discipline pupils whose behaviour is unacceptable, who break the school rules or who fail to follow a reasonable instruction;
  - at any time the pupil is in school or elsewhere;
  - in certain circumstances when a pupil's misbehaviour occurs outside of school.
- power to impose detention outside school hours;
- power to confiscate pupils' property.

The power also applies to all paid staff (unless the head teacher says otherwise) with responsibility for pupils, such as Teaching Assistants under the charge of a teacher, including on school visits.

The use of reasonable force

On rare occasions school staff may find it is necessary to use 'reasonable force' to restrain a pupil.

The DfE gives guidance for school leaders, staff and governing bodies regarding the use of reasonable force.

What is reasonable force?

The term 'reasonable force' covers the broad range of actions used by most teachers at some point in their career that involve a degree of physical contact with pupils.

Force is usually used either to control or restrain. This can range from guiding a pupil to safety by holding his or her arm, through to more extreme circumstances such as breaking up a fight or where a student needs to be restrained to prevent violence or injury.

'Reasonable in the circumstances' means using no more force than is needed.

Schools generally use force to control pupils and to restrain them. **Control** means either passive physical contact, such as standing between pupils or blocking a pupil's path, or active physical contact such as leading a pupil by the arm out of a classroom.

Restraint means to hold back physically or to bring a pupil under control. It is typically used in more extreme circumstances, for example when two pupils are fighting and refuse to separate without physical intervention.

School staff should always try to avoid acting in a way that might cause injury.

Who can use reasonable force?

All members of school staff have a legal power to use reasonable force.

Schools can use reasonable force to:

- remove disruptive children from the classroom where they have refused to follow an instruction to do so;
- prevent a pupil behaving in a way that disrupts a school event or a school trip or visit;
- prevent a pupil leaving the classroom where allowing the pupil to leave would risk their safety or lead to behaviour that disrupts the behaviour of others; and
- prevent a pupil from attacking a member of staff or another pupil, or to stop a fight in the playground.

Schools cannot:

- use force as a punishment – **it is always unlawful to use force as a punishment.**

Schools should **not** have a 'no contact' policy. There is a real risk that such a policy might place a member of staff in breach of their duty of care towards a pupil, or prevent them taking action needed to prevent a pupil causing harm (www.gov.uk/government/ uk/useofreasonableforceinschool).

Physical intervention or restraint is not a substitute for good discipline. Its use should only be as a last resort: it should be rare and it should never become habitual or routine.

- Schools should have a policy on physical intervention, cross-referenced to other relevant policies (SEN, Health and Safety, Behaviour, Child Protection).
- The school policy should help staff to develop their understanding of the appropriate use of physical restraint, update restraint training, apply alternative defusing techniques and record an incident of physical intervention appropriately.
- All physical intervention training should be set within the context of skilled behaviour management, defusing techniques and conflict resolution.
- If a school assesses that there is likelihood that physical restraint will take place, training is imperative, at least for key staff members.
- Training should not be a one-off; it should involve regular refresher courses.
- Interventions of any kind, physical or not, always require that staff take into account the age, developmental level, understanding and cultural background of the child concerned.

- Planned physical intervention is not an act of aggression or anger. **Any force, beyond what is needed to prevent harm or injury to the child or others, is unreasonable.**
- Restraint must be of minimum force to prevent further danger to the pupil, peers and adults.
- The subject should be reminded that the restraint is only temporary and clear instructions should be given as to what needs to be done in order to stop the intervention.
- Another member of staff should be present, not only to assist, but also to witness the incident and report on it afterwards. To this end staff should not be in situations that leave them alone in difficult circumstances.
- The use of seclusion is not appropriate. It is an offence to lock a child in a room without a court order.
- In educational settings, double or high door handles can be used, or outside doors can be locked, for safety or security reasons when an adult is supervising.

Section 2

Whole-school approaches

3   Whole-school thinking

A whole-school focus on promoting positive behaviour is the most effective way of reducing barriers to learning.

- School is a complex social community and has an important role to play in the development of positive behaviour models; whole-school behaviour policies should be developed with an emphasis on positive strategies.
- Policies and practice should unite staff in a common ethos in which all individuals feel supported when faced with challenges.
- Head teachers and senior leaders are responsible for creating the conditions for establishing and maintaining discipline policies in schools.
- Curriculum content and how it is delivered are very important influences on pupil's behaviour.
- Involving parents, pupils, ancillary staff and governors develops and maintains good behaviour and positive relationships in and around school.

4 Whole-school issues

Is there a whole-school behaviour policy in place?	All staff understand and support the policy.
Is there a system in place to identify and support pupils with social and emotional difficulties?	All staff are trained to recognise potential social and emotional difficulties and know how to support these pupils.
What are people focusing on – problems or solutions?	Focusing on solutions is more constructive and more likely to bring about change.
Is there a climate of positive relationships within the classroom?	Teachers and teaching assistants have high expectations and mutual respect with their pupils.
Is everyone in the school clear about school policy and the current system of rewards and sanctions?	A supply teacher coming into the school can easily understand and follow the system.
Is every member of staff helping the senior management team to lead effectively?	Everyone has a responsibility to work towards positive behaviour; enthusiasm, commitment and communication are all necessary ingredients.
Do you talk as a staff team about long-term solutions as well as short-term responses?	Creative thinking about how to prevent similar difficulties arising in the future is helpful.
Do all members of staff feel well supported?	Staff problem-solve jointly and support each other when under pressure.
Are there good relationships between pupils, staff, support staff, parents, governors and the community?	Effective communication systems are established and all parties 'buy into' the school ethos.
Is there access to training, coaching, mentoring – with ongoing support?	An effective leadership team ensures colleagues are appropriately skilled and translate this into their everyday practice.
Are staff given time to plan, review and reflect on approaches and programmes to support pupils?	Opportunities to share ideas and experiences, evaluate the effectiveness of different strategies and learn from each other are essential to development.

5   Developing a behaviour policy

A behaviour policy is a statutory requirement and must be published on the school website (https://www.gov.uk/guidance/what-maintained-schools-must-publish-online).

Many schools use either a local authority or a commercial policy template to ensure that all of the statutory elements have been addressed. A policy must articulate and reflect the ethos and core values of the school. Successful schools regularly revisit their core values with children and staff. Parents/carers and partners of the school should be familiar with the school's ethos. It should be embodied in the daily life of the school. Good schools 'walk the walk not just talk the talk'. Example policies can be found in the appendices.

When developing a school behaviour policy the following government guidance will be useful.

The law says that in maintained schools the head teacher must set out measures in the behaviour policy which aim to:

- promote good behaviour, self-discipline and respect;
- prevent bullying;
- ensure that pupils complete assigned work;
- regulate the conduct of pupils.

The head teacher must have regard to any guidance or notification provided by the governing body, which may include the following:

- screening and searching pupils;
- the power to use reasonable force and other physical contact;
- the power to discipline beyond the school gate;
- when to work with other local agencies to assess the needs of pupils who display continuous disruptive behaviour;
- pastoral care for staff accused of misconduct.

The head teacher must decide the standard of behaviour expected of pupils.

Some key aspects of school practice contribute to improving the quality of pupil behaviour – when they are clearly understood by staff, parents and pupils and are consistently applied:

- consistency in approaches to behaviour management;
- strong school leadership;
- effective classroom management;
- rewards and sanctions that are appropriately deployed;
- the modelling and teaching of good behaviour;
- staff development and support;
- pupil support systems;
- liaison with parents and other agencies;
- managing pupil transition.

The behaviour policy should acknowledge the school's legal duties under the Equality Act 2010, in respect of safeguarding and in respect of pupils with special educational needs.

6 Restorative Practices

Restorative Practices philosophy statement

Effective Restorative Practices foster awareness of how others have been affected by inappropriate behaviour. This is done by actively engaging participants in a process that separates the deed from the doer and rejects the act not the actor, allowing participators to make amends for the harm caused. Restorative Practices acknowledge the intrinsic worth of the person and their potential contribution to the school community.

The following describes a school that uses Restorative Practices to create an environment in which pupils and staff feel part of a caring community where learning can take place.

The process

Restorative Practices were instigated by the head teacher and a programme of training was undertaken by all staff in the school, this included teaching staff, teachers' aides, lunchtime supervisors, caretakers, office staff, cleaners, regular volunteers and students. It is essential that there is a whole-school commitment to the process.

A 'morning circle' is held every day for members of staff, which is intended to give opportunities for staff to know more about each other, to raise issues and solve problems.

The school has an established code of conduct, which is understood by all pupils.

At the beginning of each school year work is done to build the school community.

> *Feelings are shared. The environment is safe and supportive, feelings are acknowledged and support given. The community become aware of other's needs.*
>
> (Costell et al., 2009)

The Foundation Stage pupils will discuss feelings and develop an understanding of the consequences of their actions. Older children will build their community by setting their expectations for conduct by fellow class members. This will be followed by decisions about learning, i.e. what topics will be covered, the key questions to be answered, how they will learn in order to give ownership to their learning.

If inappropriate behaviour occurs, i.e. that which causes upset to any member of staff or pupil, a circle will be convened to discuss the issues.

> *Circles make it possible to respond to the problem, air feelings, repair the harm, address issues and plan changes for the future.*
>
> (Costell et al., 2009)

The circle may be varied in size but would include:

- the pupil or staff member who feels wronged;
- the pupil who has demonstrated the undesired behaviour;
- any pupils who may have been caught up in the incident;
- an appropriate member of staff.

The pupil will then be made accountable for their actions; all those involved will contribute ideas on how to put things right, and consequences will be agreed upon. Prompt cards can be used to support the asking of questions. Pupils with English as a second language or with special educational needs will be supported through sign language etc. An incident occurring at lunchtime will be dealt with by lunchtime supervisors so that problems do not spill over into afternoon teaching sessions.

In parallel, other ways of promoting positive behaviour are in place, including:

- whole-school star charts;
- class star charts;
- merit assemblies;
- attendance awards;
- core value awards;
- comments and awards made to individuals for behaving well.

Advice about developing Restorative Practices can be gained from the **Hull Centre for Restorative Practice** (www.hullcentreforrestorativepractice.co.uk).

All the year six pupils wear an Ambassador badge to show that they are there to support the younger children and to help sort out problems.

A teacher says:

At our school we think restoratively. If we have a problem we sort it out with a restorative circle. Restorative Practice helps our school community. In a restorative practice circle we give the person who has been hurt a chance to say what has happened to them and to say how they are feeling.

In our school we use affective statements to show how we feel in an appreciative way and when we are upset or sad. We try to be respectful and listen to others. Restorative Practice helps us to become responsible for our own behaviour.

Section 3

Putting policies into practice to create a positive learning environment

7 Providing a positive learning environment

Early years

When working with young children, adults need to create a caring environment of support, encouragement and acceptance. We should ensure understanding of the children through observation and conversation with their parents and the children themselves. Whatever the issue being dealt with, it is essential that the adult remains calm, separates the behaviour from the child and helps them to move to more positive behaviour. It may take time to improve a situation.

Perceived difficulties Children who are reluctant to follow instructions	Children's co-operation needs to be gained while allowing them to develop a sense of independence. **Strategies** • Develop simple group rules to which the children contribute and understand. • Use visual timetables to structure a session. • Ensure the child is able to understand a given request. • Give the child's name first before the request. • Back up verbal instructions with visual cues, e.g. 'Come and sit here, please' together with patting the chair seat where the child has been asked to sit. • Model appropriate behaviour. • Praise pupils who are following instructions. • Treat the child in a calm manner. • Offer choices to allow them to have some control of their environment (e.g. choice of activity). Use practical objects or pictures to support choice making (especially if a child has communication difficulties). • Give small rewards, e.g. stamps/stickers to encourage the following of instructions.
Difficulties with communication skills: • poor eye contact • lack of understanding (receptive language difficulties)	• Observe the child; try to determine the language the child uses. • Verbally label objects in the setting in a simple form, e.g. car, teddy. Moving on to adding another word, e.g. blue car, big teddy. • Provide activities to improve expressive language; work in categories, e.g. family, foods, clothes, toys,

• very limited expressive language • difficulty following routines • difficulty interacting with others	building up a few words at a time. Try feely bags, matching games, playing games in situ, i.e. in the shop, role play area. Play matching games. Use books that are at the appropriate level for the child to label objects. • Provide activities to develop receptive language in a hierarchical manner: 'Pass me the teddy… Put the biscuit on the plate… Put teddy in bed' (giving a choice of teddy/doll and bed/chair). • Support routines with visual timetables. • Model what is expected, e.g. sitting for snack time. If concerns continue seek advice from a speech and language therapist (after consulting with parents).
Tantrums	• Observe the child, try to identify if there is a reason or pattern for outbursts. • Ignore the behaviour, if possible, and praise appropriate behaviour (be explicit about what you are pleased about). • Avoid children using tantrums to manipulate adults by giving the attention they want in more acceptable ways. • Provide opportunities for physical outlets: e.g. chance to run around; balls to kick. • Play calming music. • Use puppets etc. to explore feelings and encourage children to talk about what makes us sad, cross etc.
Difficulty playing with others	• Teach them how to play with other children by modelling. Start with the adult and child playing with such activities as small world play then extend to including another child in the play. • Play turn-taking activities (with adult support), e.g. roller ball games, simple board games. • Support role play in a pretend cafe or shop. • Develop circle time activities. • Model how to join in an established friendship group, e.g. 'Can I play with you?'
Biting or hitting: can happen when the child is under pressure, is angry, excited, needs more personal space, is unable to share a toy or does not have the language to express him/herself	• Observe to identify the triggers then try to avoid these situations. If this is not possible, intervene and redirect the child, without giving too much attention. • Say 'stop' and explain that Jon is crying because biting hurts. • Teach the child a better way to communicate, maybe a hand raised to say 'stop' if they do not want another child to do something. If the child has verbal skills give them the words: 'Will you play with me?' 'Can I play with that car?' 'I am cross.' 'Please can you give me more space?' etc.

	• Teach the child to come to the adult if they have tried to resolve the situation but can't. • Praise the child for playing appropriately, especially when they are in situations in which they used to bite or when they are with particular children whom they have previously bitten.
Some children with disabilities or learning difficulties, e.g. Down's syndrome, can show behaviour that is characteristic of much younger children	• Adapt the level of support, language and expectations in response to the child's difficulties. • Provide developmentally appropriate equipment and activities.
Children with co-ordination difficulties	• Observe in different areas to determine whether it is an overall problem requiring intervention. • Encourage children to join in gross motor activities (supervision may be needed if the child lacks a sense of danger). • Give support and encouragement to take part in activities that will help to develop fine motor skills.
Children who are totally engrossed in their own play can sometimes unwittingly disrupt others, e.g. taking up all the space or knocking something over	• Draw the child's attention to this and talk to him/her about it. • Consider the room and space required for various activities.
Children who deliberately disrespect property	This may indicate unhappiness and a lack of commitment or belonging to the setting. • Observe the child and discuss with them. • Teach the correct way to use equipment. If this continues, speak to the parents to gain clues as to why the child behaves in this way and to discuss the most appropriate way forward.
Short attention/concentration span	• Select shorter stories and books that have very visual features, e.g. pop-up pictures. • Use objects that children can hold, e.g. from story sacks. These will help to hold their interest. • Turning the pages of the book may help to maintain attention. • Each child holds an object from a story, e.g. the foods from *The Hungry Caterpillar*, and has to listen for the name of his/her object to be read out and place it in an appropriate place. • Short tasks, which are built up in length as the child's concentration improves.

	• Encourage them to sit to complete a task rather than standing.
	• 'Engineering' to finish a task, e.g. the adult puts in some jigsaw pieces and the child puts in the last one, so that the child perceives that he/she has finished it.
	• Praise for completing a task.
Inappropriate use of language	• Observe and discuss the issues with parents.
	• Use stories that educate children on issues like racism or sexism, e.g. *Skin I'm In* by Pat Thomas.
	• Use a simple social story to explain that some words are never used at school.
Attention-seeking – Adult attention is vital for children's physical and emotional wellbeing. Some children constantly seek adult attention.	• Give praise and attention for positive reasons. Catch them being good.
Quiet/withdrawn children – These children can easily be overlooked. Observation will help to decide if the quietness is caused by fear, distress or a lack of self-esteem.	• Discuss with parents/carers to establish if the behaviour is across all settings or not.
	• Unusually quiet or passive children require just as much consideration as the child who is attention-seeking.
	• Encourage interaction with adults and peers by setting up play situations, e.g. small world play, turn-taking games.

Early years: examples of rewards

Rewards to young children should be given as soon as possible after the event they are being rewarded for, so that they understand the connection. The reward should be accompanied by a simple, clear explanation of why they are being rewarded so that the child is encouraged to replicate the behaviour.

Praise and stickers or stamps provide quick rewards and EYFS settings will have their own system of acknowledging good behaviours, including those listed below.

Golden cushion: children are chosen to sit on the cushions after demonstrating some feature of good behaviour or special trait.

Colourful kites: the pupil earns tails for his/her paper kite. Attach the tails to the string of the paper kite.

Fill the flower box: label a plastic planting trough with the words 'Beautiful Behaviour in Bloom'. The pupil earns paper flowers to put in the classroom garden.

Quick notes: or a small certificate given by the class teacher on an *ad hoc* or regular basis for any behaviour that is an achievement for a particular child.

Reward cards of varying types: apple trees, ladybirds, dinosaurs with outlines for spots to be put on. These are given when the pupil carries out the required, agreed behaviour.

Rewards can also be tied into the class topic, e.g. put another wheel on the train if the topic is transport.

Helper of the day: he/she could have his/her photograph placed on the wall.
Star of the day: a particular pupil's photograph is displayed in a 'frame' with a comment underneath stating why he/she is a star. The credit could be given for being especially kind to another child, for sharing equipment or listening well. The whole class could make suggestions or the teacher could make the choice.

All of these strategies (especially the last two) are effective in raising a child's self-esteem.

Some teachers find the Pinterest website useful in gaining ideas from other teachers.

8 Providing an effective learning environment

Primary and secondary provision

In order to assist a pupil to succeed within the classroom environment, key aspects of organisation and delivery should be considered, bearing in mind that pupils with social and emotional difficulties benefit from appropriate structure and organisation.

The physical arrangement of the classroom

- Ensure the layout of classroom is visually obvious: it should be clear where the pupil should sit, stand, wait/queue.
- Be aware of potential distractions within and around the classroom and attempt to minimise them.
  - noisy heating appliances;
  - high-traffic areas;
  - doors or windows;
  - over-stimulating displays;
  - flickering/bright lights;
  - strong sunlight.
- Reduce clutter and provide a clear working environment.
- Ensure learning displays, e.g. word lists, are accessible.
- Have learning resources immediately available at the start of each lesson.
- Ensure all materials are easily accessible and reduce the need for unnecessary movement around the room (remembering that some pupils may need to move (under direction) at regular intervals).
- Label resources clearly and appropriately to prevent the pupil 'wandering' to look for a piece of equipment or its place to put it away.
- Allow the pupil to be in charge of their own equipment as far as possible.
- Some pupils may feel the need to 'escape' from the room, this could be an agreed plan between the pupil and teacher allowing him/her to go to a designated area containing books (or alternative) for a calming time before returning to the teaching area.

General classroom organisation

- Structure and consistent routines are essential to bring about desirable behavioural responses from all pupils.

- When changes in routine are unavoidable, inform pupils in advance; if this is not possible, an appropriate explanation should be given and any new arrangements clearly explained.
- Consider the best place for the pupil to sit during lesson e.g.:
  - at the front so that there is less distraction ahead;
  - close to the teacher (to be seen as a privilege rather than a punishment) to enable easy and discreet observation, reinforce instructions and give immediate praise and feedback;
  - next to a good role model (particularly one who is seen as having good 'street cred');
  - away from pupils who have the potential to distract;
  - near to the door if there is a need to move if short breaks are required.

- Try to integrate rather than isolate.
- Pupils with autism may benefit from an individual work space.
- Have materials that the pupil likes/engages in as a back-up in case he/she is having a very bad day and cannot access the learning materials in the lesson.
- Use visual support and structure to assist the pupils in organising the learning tasks, e.g. symbol timetable, egg timer, written lists, work trays.

Around and about school

All staff need to ensure that pupils are appropriately supervised in their classrooms, cloakrooms, when they are moving around school, when they are coming in from, and going out to the playground and when they are visiting places outside school.

One Year 6 teacher's perspective on behaviour in the classroom

She has high expectations for behaviour:

- learning should take place;
- children should get along with each other;
- we should build communities;
- children should take responsibility and control their own behaviour.

To achieve this she uses:

- problem solving circle time;
- consistency of approach;
- modelling good behaviour by using good role models;
- the use of raffle tickets as rewards for good attitudes, behaviour, work, kindness to others;
- rewards of marbles in the jar for good team work;
- the incentive of receiving 'Golden Time' at the end of the week;
- building a positive community in her classroom.

Power vacuum

I've come to the frightening conclusion that I am the decisive element in the classroom.

It's my personal approach that creates the climate; it's my daily mood that makes the weather.

As a teacher I possess a tremendous power to make a child's life miserable or joyous.

I can be a tool of torture or an instrument of inspiration.

I can humiliate or humour, hurt or heal.

In all situations, it is my response that decides whether a crisis will be escalated or de-escalated and a child humanised or de-humanised.

Halm Ginott

9 Lesson activity and delivery

Consider the following when planning and delivering lessons:

- Ensure that pupils understand what is expected of them and the purpose of a lesson.
- Outline the content and the structure of the school day, and the learning objectives and success criteria of each lesson.
- Use regular, unambiguous reminders of behavioural expectations.
- Use observations/assessments to *ensure work is at the appropriate level* and provides appropriate challenge to prevent frustration and subsequent undesired behaviour.
- Ensure the lesson activity is meaningful and enjoyable for the pupil and will promote success.
- Personalise the learning resources to something of a high interest to the particular pupil until he/she is ready to participate in general classroom work.
- Teach the pupil how to ask for help, devise a discrete signal, e.g. a coloured pen or symbol placed on the table that indicates that he/she requires support.
- If the pupil struggles with sitting and concentrating for long periods build in a physical challenge/task to the activity – this could be as simple as going to collect items, or employing 'brain gym' activities.
- Chunk the activity into different parts.
- Encourage peer tutoring and co-operative/collaborative working.
- Assign specific roles when employing a co-operative learning approach (some pupils may need support to work co-operatively).
- Assist pupils with organising their work; provide clearly marked trays for unfinished and completed work.
- Build on pupils' successes from previous lessons.
- Remember that pupils who have behavioural difficulties may also have difficulty holding and manipulating information in their working memory. This will clearly impact on behaviour, motivation and concentration and needs to be acknowledged and catered for, e.g. by providing picture cues, lists, Post-it notes.
- Use a multi-sensory format when delivering lessons.

10 Communication

Many pupils with emotional and social behavioural difficulties have communication scores more than two years below chronological ages, resulting in serious problems when attempting to follow instructions. They may also be poor at reading body language, so miss a lot of a teacher's non-verbal communication.

Two thirds of 7–14 year olds with serious behaviour problems have language impairment.

(The Communication Trust, thecommunicationtrust.or.uk/
media/402037/importance-of-communication-skills.pdf)

Consider the following when communicating with pupils

- Use visual prompts to support verbal communication.
- Say the pupil's name first if giving an individual instruction.
- Keep instructions clear and simple. Try to avoid multiple commands.
- Ensure pupils understand the task/activity by asking them to repeat back or demonstrate what they should be doing rather than asking 'Do you understand?' and taking a nod or 'yes' as a sign of their understanding.
- Maintain good eye contact during verbal instruction.
- Provide regular, precise, positive feedback on their engagement in the task, e.g. 'John, that's good listening.'
- Help the pupil feel comfortable when seeking additional clarification. Repeat instructions in a calm and positive manner when required.
- Give visual prompts, e.g. Post-it notes, desk prompts as reminders of appropriate behaviour.
- Break activities down into manageable stages so that only one piece of information needs to be processed at a time. When one stage has been completed successfully, the next stage can then be presented.
- Ensure pupils have understood and correctly written down their homework.
- If a pupil appears to repeatedly have difficulty following instructions, seek further advice from the SENCo. It could be that he or she has other needs that require support.

11 Creating a positive environment

General whole class strategies

The guidelines and strategies as outlined in the school's behaviour policy should be followed by all members of staff.

- As pupils move to a new classroom at the beginning of a school year they should be explicitly taught the new expectations within the classroom, e.g. where they line up, where they sit etc.
- At the beginning of a term agree with the pupils a limited number of clear and achievable classroom rules. Ensure that all the pupils understand them.
- Also set rules for behaviour outside the classroom.
- All rules need to be clear and concise. Examples of keeping the rules should be modelled regularly and reinforced, not just highlighted at times of crisis.
- Display these rules in the classroom: use photographs, symbols and/or text.
- Praise the specific behaviour, e.g. 'I liked the way you put your hand up when you knew the answers', rather than 'good boy' or 'well done'.
- Remind a pupil of the expected behaviour, rather than pointing out their negative actions, e.g. instead of 'Stop shouting out the answers', say 'Put up your hand'.
- Ensure that work is at the appropriate level for the pupil, to avoid frustration and possible inappropriate behaviour occurring as well as damage to self-esteem.
- Introduce a 'Feelings Chart'. This consists of a photograph of each pupil together with a series of labels describing different feelings (with a picture and writing); happy, sad, angry, tired, worried, hungry. The pupils match the appropriate label to their picture. This can indicate to the teacher that intervention may be required.
- A circle time in the morning could be led by the teacher or a pupil. This could simply be to ask 'Are you OK today, Jim?' and hopefully the reply would be, 'I am OK thank you, Paul.' If the answer is in the negative the pupil could be offered a support partner for the day.
- Establish ways of preparing the class to listen:

  - play a recognised song/piece of music to indicate that it is time to tidy up or get ready to listen (the pupils can choose the song);
  - countdown from 10/5 to 1;
  - use visual actions, e.g. copy a clapping rhythm;
  - give a signal, e.g. a hand in the air;
  - praise the pupils who are listening;
  - change the activities to keep it fresh.

- Praise good behaviour and work frequently, to ensure motivation and task appliance.
- Any reward helps pupils appreciate how achievements are helped by their own attitude and effort:
  - a non-verbal sign – a smile, nod, thumbs up!
  - praise – quiet, personal praise or public – in class, assemblies etc.;
  - from elsewhere (head, deputy head, Phase Leader);
  - stars, stickers, points, certificates, letters, privileges (but no sweets);
  - examples of very good behaviour can be brought to pupils' attention in assemblies;
  - a note, email or text to parents reporting good behaviour.

- There should be an appropriate balance between praise/rewards and sanctions. As a rule of thumb, try to praise pupils at least three times as often as we censure them. There should be flexibility shown in the use of rewards and sanctions to take account of individual pupil circumstances.
- Concrete rewards are usually more effective, as these offer a tangible reminder to the pupil of how well he/she is doing, e.g. a star chart or tokens that can be exchanged at a later time for a favourite activity or treat.
- Give pupils a chance to redeem themselves, e.g. if using a traffic light, give them a chance to go from red to amber if they make the correct choices. Keeping them on red for a long time and gaining no rewards, serves no purpose, as they see no reason to be 'good'.
- Deal with undesirable behaviour from close proximity rather than from across the room, to avoid disrupting the rest of the class and highlighting the pupil.
- Avoid confrontation and strategies that allow the pupil to gain an audience.
- Be firm rather than aggressive, shouting is unacceptable – avoid idle threats.
- Listen: establish the facts.
- Find out if the pupil is aware that the behaviour is unacceptable and whether he/she knows the effect it has on others.
- Encourage the pupil to think of, or offer alternative types of behaviour.
- Use sanction sparingly – in very small steps and build redemption into any sanction.

Avoid whole-class 'blanket' sanctions.

12 Play/breaktimes and lunchtimes

Many pupils find it difficult to maintain appropriate behaviour during unstructured times such as lunch and break time. For these pupils it can help to provide opportunities for less troublesome breaks, which consequently allow them to return to lessons in a calm manner.

Lunchtime supervisors may require training in appropriate ways to deal with pupils. They should be aware of current good practice exercised within the school and be aware of relevant school policies, including Child Protection and anti-bullying.

Suggestions to support primary pupils

- Break down the lunchtime break into smaller components, with appropriate behaviour rewarded, e.g. 15 minutes helping a teacher to do a job, a short time to play football, time for lunch, followed by structured play.
- Provide activities such as lunchtime clubs to play table-top games.
- Structured outdoor games organised by dinner supervisors or support assistants should help to improve playground behaviour (with extra support for pupils who need help to learn the rules and be guided in their behaviour).
- Peer monitoring or 'buddy' systems for younger pupils may help to guide pupils to purposeful activities in the playground.

An example of good practice at lunchtime comes from a large Hull primary school and is as follows.

The Wellbeing staff meet with Dinner Supervisors (some of whom are Teaching Assistants within the school). They discuss any pertinent issues and name any children in need of extra support.

The two members of staff mix with the children during the lunch break, know all their names and have therefore built a good trusting relationship with the children. Any child with a problem feels comfortable enough to talk about something that is concerning them and solutions can be sought. Some children prefer to write a note, knowing that support will follow.

There are designated Play Leaders (again Teaching Assistants within the school) who will organise games with those who want to play.

Some Year 5 and 6 pupils are trained to be Playground Buddies. They are easily visible in their bright red fleeces and will spot any children who look as though they need a friend to play with. There is also a 'Buddy bus stop' where children can sit if they want to play and the Buddies will engage them in play.

The Dinner Supervisors and Playground Buddies will try to resolve any issues that occur at lunchtime through a 'quick circle', which involves asking questions:

1   What happened?
2   How do you feel?
3   How can we make it better?

Hopefully, problems can be solved rather than spilling into the afternoon lessons. If not, the Wellbeing staff hold a more in-depth meeting later on.

The school offers a number of clubs at lunchtime, which last for half an hour, and include:

- an art club;
- Lego therapy: a group initiated by the Northcott Autism Outreach Team, and intended for pupils who struggle with social interaction in the playground;
- a choir;
- a Dinosaur Club;
- a Gymnastics Club;
- a Football Club for boys and girls, which is run by a football coach and attendance is only through good behaviour in class (a very good incentive!).

Suggestions to support secondary pupils at breaktimes

- Consider any appropriate strategies from above.
- Some pupils may require a space to retreat to at lunchtime where they can be quiet or seek out the company of a support assistant.
- Some pupils may benefit from an area where there are fewer pupils around but which gives opportunities for card games, computer games to take place, supervised by older pupils or learning mentors who could support and extend social skills.
- The availability of lunchtime clubs (e.g. computer clubs) would provide areas away from the main body of pupils, but may again, need some support for pupils to access the activities successfully.

13 Gender difference

There is growing research to suggest that there are psychological differences between boys and girls that affect the way in which they think, behave and communicate. Obviously the influence of parents is significant but it is thought that gender differences are present from a child's very early days.

The differences tend to impact on behaviour within the classroom in several ways.

Boys...	Girls...
play more active games: riding bikes, ball games	often enjoy quieter games: drawing, imaginative play
lack fine motor control required for writing	develop fine motor skills more easily
are slower, as young children, to develop communication skills, which has a consequence for developing literacy skills	on the whole develop language skills more quickly
are disadvantaged with the above resulting in a possible lack of confidence and motivation in this area	develop literacy skills more readily and can be more confident
interrupt and answer more often (even if they don't know the answer)	talk less in a class situation but are better at articulating their feelings
often act first and think later	plan and organise their work more effectively
tend to overestimate their abilities	tend to underestimate their skills and work harder to compensate

There are twice as many boys with learning difficulties than girls and four times as many boys with autism than girls.

The following points, whilst avoiding stereotyping, may be considered as strategies to support boys to learn more effectively.

- Encourage them to express themselves verbally; give support for role play, circle times, friendship groups, giving them the skills to communicate, develop relationships and avoid or at least resolve conflict.
- Provide opportunities for physical activities rather than having too much sedentary work.
- Give guidance to take part in activities to develop fine motor skills, with use of ICT to record work in order to maintain self-esteem.
- Develop an enjoyment of reading through use of male-orientated reading material, including examples of non-fiction.
- Give extra support to master the use of written language, e.g. mind mapping to help structure work.
- Provide good role models: members of staff, community members, older students, celebrity/sports figures.
- Have teaching staff as role models who engage with boys and who enthuse about learning to try to overcome the boys attitude of it not being 'cool' to learn.
- Ensure that boys' expectations that teachers are firm but fair are upheld.
- Set challenges and create problem solving situations.
- Set targets and allow the boys to be part of setting them.
- Working in mixed pairings/small groups helps to prevent male domination, encourages females to speak and allows for planning skills to be developed.

All the above together with encouragement and praise for achievement should help to prevent disaffection, help to develop learning skills and encourage self-esteem.

Section 4

Support staff

14   Support staff

Working in the classroom

The Special Educational Needs and Disability Code of Practice, 2014 states:

> Where the interventions involve group or one-to-one teaching away from the main class or subject teacher, teaching staff should **still retain responsibility for the pupil**, working closely with any teaching assistants or specialist staff involved.

Guidelines for support staff

- Direct pupils' attention to the teacher rather than them expecting you (the Teaching Assistant) to listen **for** them.
- Encourage pupils to start tasks immediately.
- Reinforce the teacher's instructions, either verbally or with writing prompts.
- Interpret, reinforce and repeat instructions if necessary.
- Encourage pupils to stay on task by giving plentiful praise and rewards.
- Encourage and redirect pupils back to the task in hand if their attention wanders.
- Reinforce good behaviour positively by using plenty of smiles and nods.
- Use humour, never sarcasm: keep the tone of your voice calm and comments positive.
- Acknowledge even the smallest achievement made by a pupil.
- Look at the group at regular intervals to check behaviour (there will be a need to check more in less-structured time when pupils have less guidance).
- Check the behaviour of the child when working/playing alone. They may choose to have some 'space' or may require some intervention in order to play with others.
- Observe the behaviour of pupils working/playing in a group. If they are unable to sort any difficulties, intervene.
- Look for triggers that indicate why a pupil is behaving in a particular way, rather than reacting to a behaviour. Looking at what has contributed to a disturbance may help to stop it happening again.
- Try to step in quickly in a quiet, calm way if behaviour starts to go badly.
- Anticipate where things may go wrong and try to move the pupil on to another activity.
- Try to create a rhythm or a particular pace that feels comfortable for all (the pupil, the group and you).
- Learn to recognise when to step in and speak to a pupil and when to leave it to the teacher. Sometimes stepping in will disturb the lesson.
- Make sure pupils are treated in the same way. Avoid favouring the pupil you work with, or being harder on him/her than others in the class.
- Try to respond in the same way each time, and in the way the pupil would expect.

Ultimately, management of behaviour is the responsibility of the teacher.

Using visual cues

Visual cues are useful for pupils who become confused by, or who do not understand, verbal instructions. These can take the form of timetables, cue cards, desk sequences, reminders on the blackboard of work to be done or ticks to show good behaviour.

- A learning task task can be given in a visual way as well as a verbal one.
- Lists or pictures on the board or on charts can show pupils how to get on with their work.
- Showing that behaviour is right or wrong can be done non-verbally. For example:
    - smiling, frowning, giving a nod, thumbs up; shaking the head – these gestures draw less attention to the pupil than verbal comments;
    - eye gaze (eye contact for a long time) can show the pupil that he/she should change his/her behaviour;
    - standing next to the pupil can be used to indicate that you have noticed the pupil;
    - visual cue cards and other visual aids may be used for pupils who need more than just gestures. These may be designed and made by the pupil and can show good sitting, good listening etc.

15 Support staff

Guidelines for working with pupils

Teachers and Teaching Assistants may consider the following:

Do...	Try to avoid...
help the child see his/her mistake and how to overcome it.	asking the pupil 'Why did you do that?' when they don't know themselves.
tell the pupil what you would like him/her to do.	telling the pupil what you **don't** want him to do.
look for answers to the pupil's unwanted behaviour.	concentrating on the pupil's misbehaviours or problems all the time.
sidestep confrontations whenever possible.	getting into an argument with the pupil.
attempt to offer choices.	insisting on only one type of work from the pupil.
provide a clear, predictable learning environment.	cluttered areas.
show that you like and respect the pupil even when you don't like his/her behaviour.	socially rejecting the pupil.
ensure instructions are at the appropriate level and goals are achievable.	making unrealistic demands on the pupil.
give the pupil opportunities to develop choice-making skills.	making all the decisions for the pupil.
encourage independent behaviour and work.	encouraging dependence on support staff.
work with other pupils while keeping an eye on the pupil you are assigned to.	sitting next to the pupil at all times.
encourage interaction with peers or allow the pupil to be solitary, as appropriate.	offering too close an oversight during breaks and lunchtimes.

Do...	Try to avoid...
encourage the pupil to be independent, e.g. ensuring drawers are clearly labelled.	collecting equipment for the pupil or putting it away.
ensure work is at an appropriate level and can be carried out with minimal support (note any support given).	completing a task for a pupil.
give short instructions at the pupil's level of development, with visual prompts.	using language inappropriate for the pupil.
make sure that the pupil knows what to do. Expect a task to be completed.	making unnecessary allowances for the pupil.
observe the pupil: determine reasons for behaviour and consider if changes can be made.	tolerating undesirable behaviour.

Section 5

Pupils and parents

16 The voice of the pupil

The SEN and Disability Code of Practice states that:

> Children have a right to be involved in making decisions and exercising choices. They have a right to receive and impart information, to express an opinion, and to have that opinion taken into account in any matters affecting them. Their views should be given due weight according to their age, maturity and capability.
>
> (Articles 12 and 13 of the United Nations Convention on the Rights of the Child)

Pupils need to be included in decision-making because:

- Children have equal rights to participate in discussions that will affect their future.
- Children have the right to express their own points of view even if these contradict those of others.
- School systems, particularly the SEN and exclusionary systems, can often contribute to the creation of a negative identity for the child.
- People need to understand issues from the child's point of view, when making decisions and developing effective strategies.
- If children are not included they will have no investment in what is taking place.

Strategies for including the pupil's point of view

- Pupils should contribute to developing the school's ethos and policies.
- Ensure that adults are positive and solution-focused.
- Listen to children and young people and include them in meetings about themselves, e.g. planning meetings, reviews and monitoring IEPs. (Be aware that a pupil may disclose something that is a Child Protection issue. All staff must be clear about the school's Child Protection policy.)
- Use a 'Restorative Practice' approach to allow pupils a voice with staff and peers in order to include them in resolving a problem rather than just administering a sanction for their misdemeanour.
- Use a 'One Page Profile' to allow pupils to give a picture of themselves.
- Use an advocate if pupils find meetings intimidating.
- Help pupils write what they wish to say if this is easier for them.
- Use peer advisers or peer groups to promote pupil participation.
- Ensure that children and young people understand exactly, what the issues are.
- Establish a school council.

17 Developing self-esteem

The Oxford Dictionary's definition of self-esteem is... 'Confidence in one's own worth or abilities.'

> A child's ability to form good relationships not only enhances their personal development but helps them progress intellectually... Equipping children to understand and articulate their own identity, take the perspectives of others, and recognise their rights and responsibilities in the social worlds they inhabit, we are preparing them to cope confidently with their own future lives and to contribute to the future of their communities.
>
> (Burrell and Riley, 2007)

High or low levels of self-esteem can affect how an individual faces new challenges and influence their feelings as a learner, towards school, their peers and their future.

Self-concept may be thought of as like an old-fashioned set of balance scales. On one side are the negative beliefs we have about ourselves; on the other, the positive ones.

These beliefs begin at an early age and are affected by our successes and failures throughout life, and by what we are told about ourselves by our parents, friends, teachers and others. Children take in and remember what they hear about themselves. 'Today's talk is tomorrow's thought.' This process will continue unless challenged by different experiences. Self-concept is powerful and can influence our performance: a child who has a poor self-concept of him/herself as a learner will not learn as effectively as one with a good self-concept, irrespective of ability levels.

The following strategies may help to build self-esteem.

- Find out as much as possible about a pupil who is causing concerns by talking to the SENCo, Phase Leader, parents and the pupil.
- Observe any difficulties they may have in behaviour and/or learning.
- If appropriate set interventions in place.
- Discuss goals with the pupil. Encourage them to set their own goals: make them attainable but appropriately challenging.
- Set work at an appropriate level. If they are working below the age-related expectations, then targets should be where they are working at, not at the chronological age.

- Language, tone and non-verbal signals used when working with children can affect their opinion of themselves, re-enforcing their opinion if negative or changing for the better, if positive.
- If opinions are asked for then listen to the pupil, value what is said and try to implement what has been suggested. If this is not possible then explain why not.
- Acknowledge and celebrate success whenever it is achieved; this could be personally, with parents or on a wider school community level.
- Celebrate good work and display it. Work can be shared in many different ways; writing, using ICT, audio recordings and video.
- Recognise strengths and build on them. Make the pupil the expert in their own area, sharing knowledge with their peers, perhaps as a peer mentor.
- Consider times which have less structure, e.g. breaktimes and lunchtimes when the pupil may have difficulty and put strategies in place. (See 'Breaktimes and lunchtimes' in Section 3). Having a positive breaktime rather than being in trouble will be better for self-esteem and allow the pupil to be ready to learn afterwards.
- Establish an effective system of praise and rewards, focusing attention on positive attributes.
- Give specific praise (e.g. 'Well done, you ignored Liam when he was...').
- Affirm positive behaviour frequently. Build success into every day, and reward immediately and generously.
- Intervene as soon as there is a hint of inappropriate behaviour, rather than letting it build.
- Give responsibility to the pupil.

It is important to note that at least three positive messages are required to balance out every single negative message, to avoid damage to a child's self-esteem.

18 Developing peer relationships

Pupils who present inappropriate behaviour due to social and emotional difficulties can easily become isolated from their peer group and community. Others may avoid them because they do not like the behaviour and do not wish to be associated with it. Being unable to develop and sustain rewarding peer relationships will impact in a negative way on the pupil's level of self-esteem.

Approaches that aim to build positive peer relationships and friendship skills:

- Develop a positive relationship with the pupil and provide a good model of behaviour.
- Make sure the pupil and his/her peers know you value them, even though you do not always like their behaviour.
- Publicly praise the pupil whenever possible.
- Provide social skills training to help develop a pupil's communication and interactive skills.
- Teach 'emotional literacy': there are many activities and programmes available to teach skills such as self-awareness, managing feelings and conflict resolution.
- Use peer mediation and listening services – these can help when friendships have broken down.
- Use solution-focused approaches such as engaging young people in developing their own goals and action plans.
- Make use of cognitive-behavioural approaches that develop children's awareness of why they react as they do, and strategies to overcome these responses, for example, anger management.
- Develop support groups and friendship groups. The no-blame approach to bullying, Restorative Practice and Circle of Friends are specific means of developing support for those with varying difficulties including those displaying bullying behaviour.
- Restorative discussions are effective in encouraging positive friendships between peers.
- Develop buddy systems in school to ensure young people are not left isolated. Sensitive classmates could be seated next to the pupil and could 'look out' for him/her and attempt to include the pupil in school activities.
- Use collaborative group work to encourage discussion – pupils learn that they have to co-operate with others in order to complete the task.
- Foster the pupil's involvement with others. Encourage active socialisation and limit time spent alone, e.g. a support assistant seated at the lunch table could encourage

the pupil to participate in the conversation of his/her peers, not only by soliciting the pupil's opinions and asking him/her questions but also by subtly reinforcing other children who do the same.

- Provide structured play opportunities, e.g. encouraging the pupil to play a board game with one or two others, not only structures play but also offers an opportunity to practise social skills such as turn-taking;
- Use curriculum-based approaches that use drama, art, creative writing and discussion to explore moral dilemmas.
- Incorporate the elements of effective communication, participation and co-operation into curriculum planning and preparation.
- Emphasise the pupil's academic strengths by creating co-operative learning situations in which reading skills, vocabulary, memory and so on may be viewed as assets by peers, thereby engendering acceptance.
- If the lesson involves pairing off or choosing partners, use some planned means of pairing rather than random choice.
- Have an effective anti-bullying policy and anti-bullying procedures.

19 Ways to develop good relationships between pupils and staff

Dealing with challenging behaviour can be time-consuming, frustrating and stressful. It is therefore vital that within school there is a supportive ethos. Senior leadership has the responsibility for building the ethos of the school, and for supporting staff in creating an inclusive and accepting climate.

Developing positive relationships between pupils and staff is also extremely important in eliciting appropriate behaviour from pupils.

- Research background information about the pupil to determine whether there is an underlying situation or condition that will influence the way in which they behave in school.
- Separate the person from the behaviour ('I like you, but not that behaviour').
- Try to see the young person holistically, not just as 'the problem' (talk to them about their interests, hopes and activities).
- Listen before putting your own point of view (it is always easier to listen to someone if you feel you have already been 'heard').
- Speak in a respectful manner (try to avoid unintentional put-downs).
- Manage your own emotions. Avoid shouting or other forms of distancing yourself from the young person (someone who is distressed has enough emotions of their own to cope with without having to cope with yours).
- Discuss with the pupil exactly what good behaviour 'looks' like for them.
- Try and elicit the desired behaviour through co-operation rather than coercion.
- Find times to provide some individual attention.
- Use humour (sensitively – humour directed at someone who cannot respond is not funny, it is bullying).

20 Anti-bullying

The following section gives an approach to identifying and dealing with any incidences of bullying.

Definition

Bullying can be described as a deliberate act done to cause distress solely in order to give a feeling of power, status or other gratification to the bully. It can include ostracising, name-calling, teasing, threats and extortion, through to physical assault on persons and/or their property. It can be an unresolved, single frightening incident that casts a shadow over a child's life, or a series of such incidents.

It is important to understand that bullying is not the odd falling-out with friends, name calling, arguments or when the occasional 'joke' is played on someone. Children and young people do sometimes fall out or say hurtful things because they are upset. When problems of this kind arise it is not necessarily classed as 'bullying' unless it is done repeatedly and on purpose.

The following is a list of reasons from *DCSF 'Safe to Learn' guidance why bullying may take place:

- appearance;
- ability;
- health;
- family or home circumstances, e.g. looked after, young carers;
- social class;
- race, religion and culture;
- disability/SEN;
- homophobia;
- sexist, sexual and transgender.

---

*DCSF was the Department for Children, Schools and Families until 2010, replaced by the DfE (Department for Education).

Physical bullying

Physically abusing the victim is often the easiest form of bullying to be recognised as it can be witnessed and reported by others, and may leave marks on the victim. It can involve intimidation by the use of larger stature or gangs, identified, for example, when they block the victim's exit and corner him or her, empty a school bag, damage homework, etc.

Verbal bullying

Verbal bullying can be the use of derogatory terms about the victim, his friends or family. It is often hard to detect because the victims tend to want to keep quiet about their ordeal.

Cyber bullying

Cyber bullying can happen at all times of the day and night, with a potentially bigger audience, and more accessories as people upload content at a click. Cyber bullying can be individual or group behaviour that includes hurtful texts, spreading rumours through social networking sites and assuming a false identity to cause harm or mischief. Ensure that good, safe IT practice is embedded in all teaching and learning.

Indirect/social bullying

Indirect bullying can take the form of using derogatory terms to abuse someone, alienating them from peers or excluding them from a group or an activity. It can be very difficult to determine when this is occurring but being stopped multiple times from joining an activity is normally a show of social bullying.

Signs of being bullied

Pupils who are being bullied may show changes in behaviour, such as becoming shy and nervous, feigning illness, taking unusual absences or clinging to adults. There may be evidence of changes in standards of work and lapses in concentration.

Prevention of bullying

Actively encourage positive relationships throughout the school and give lots of opportunities for discussions and problem-solving to take place. In addition, consider which of the strategies listed below could be effective in your class/school.

Strategies for preventing bullying
• daily check-in/out circles
• problem-solving circles
• SEAL (Social, Emotional Aspects of Learning (**//www.education.gov.uk**)
• anti-bullying awareness raising and key messages (classrooms and assemblies)
• participation in Anti-Bullying Week, special events
• behaviour rules, code of conduct

• effective supervision by staff
• a curriculum that reflects the school's ethos celebrating the rich diversity of our world
• emotional wellbeing workers
• support programmes for vulnerable pupils
• establishing a safe and secure physical environment
• involvement of pupils, for example, peer support
• Healthy Schools activities
• working with the School Council
• circle time
• playground buddies
• peaceful problem solvers

Communication with parents/carers

What to do if you think your child may be being bullied

Watch for a pattern:

- wanting more/less attention;
- not wanting to go to school;
- frequent minor illnesses;
- coming home with bruises or torn clothing;
- possessions disappearing;
- becoming withdrawn.

What to do:

- treat the matter seriously;
- keep a diary of incidents;
- try and help your child deal with the situation;
- do not approach the bully;
- do not advise your child to fight back;
- contact the school and speak to the Lead Co-ordinator, Key Worker, head teacher.

Website links to additional resources

Anti-Bullying Alliance – www.anti-bullyingalliance.org.uk
NSPCC – www.nspcc.org.uk
Childline – www.childline.org.uk
Kidscape – www.kidscape.org.uk

21　Working with parents

Early years providers, schools and colleges should fully engage parents and/or young people with SEN when drawing up policies that affect them. Enabling parents to share their knowledge about their child and engage in positive discussion helps to give them confidence that their views and contributions are valued and will be acted upon.

(Special Educational Needs and Disability Code of Practice, 2014)

The following should be considered when working with parents:

- Be aware of the differences in power between the professionals and parents.
- Avoid making parents feel disempowered, sidelined or criticised as ineffective by the school.
- Criticism of their children often arouses powerful feelings of guilt, shame and embarrassment in parents, and they might oppose or reject the school's views because of these feelings.
- Parents may have had negative experiences of school themselves and this can lead to a variety of responses, including taking their child's side against the school.
- Do not make assumptions and attributions based on the race, culture or gender of children and their families.
- Be aware that misunderstandings happen around different attitudes, beliefs, value systems and expectations.

When working with families:

- Assign members of staff to be in the playground as families arrive at and leave school. A familiar member of staff can speak in an informal manner to parents and develop relationships that can then be built on, particularly if any issues arise. In secondary schools, this informal approach is more difficult to achieve. Parents/carers may have to be invited into school for 'a chat'; make them feel as comfortable as possible in a non-intimidating environment; offer coffee; consider using a Teaching Assistant from the local community as a 'go-between'.
- Discuss any issues with parents before they become more serious. Try to think of a way forward to present to the pupil and their parent.
- Meet regularly as progress is made to reinforce appropriate behaviour.
- Avoid discussing a child's behaviour in the playground when other parents may be within hearing range.
- Avoid making negative comments about the pupil within their hearing. Pupils should not be hearing negative comments about themselves. Give positive

messages to the parent about their child; if problems arise find solutions in a productive manner. Be aware that parents do not want to fear the teacher coming to them at the end of the day!

- Be positive. Think, 'Everyone is doing their best, given their circumstances and the information available.'
- Listen to parents: they may have a different, alternative and valid perspective.
- Work collaboratively by sharing information and expertise.
- Become active partners with parents and professionals, work together to develop systems that can be used at both home and school.
- Make meetings friendly and supportive. An informal talk with a cup of tea may be a good starting point.
- Build trust and mutual respect by using informal situations to encourage dialogue. Look for solutions via other possibilities.

When parents are 'resistant' or 'won't engage'

Reasons why parents do not engage can be complex. It could be because:

- They do not feel they are being listened to.
- They do not feel they are being treated with respect.
- They are asked to do something of which they are not capable.
- They do not engage with the educational culture.
- They may have had bad experiences in school themselves.
- There may be a language barrier.

Follow the ideas suggested when working with families, if there are still difficulties:

- Make home visits (ensure Health and Safety procedures are carried out).
- Be persistent in trying to engage, don't give up.
- Be prepared to be flexible with the timing of meetings.
- Make sure good records are kept of discussions, agreements and actions taken.
- Make sure there are clear, consistent boundaries and consequences.
- Monitor progress carefully.
- Follow school procedures carefully, including those relating to discipline.
- Liaise with other agencies and services including Education Welfare and Social Care, if necessary.

Section 6

Approaches and Interventions for pupils who require an individual response

22   Observing the pupil

Carrying out a classroom observation is one way of developing a greater understanding of a pupil's behavioural strengths and difficulties. It should be carried out in conjunction with background knowledge of the pupil. Observation can be used as a way of answering specific questions such as:

- how frequently a pupil behaves in a certain way;
- how a pupil is able/unable to cope with different types of classroom organisation/ activities;
- how the pupil responds to a particular teaching style;
- whether or not the classroom tasks are appropriate in terms of the pupil's ability, cultural background and so on.

A one-off observation provides only a snapshot of how a pupil behaves in a particular lesson, on a particular day, at a particular time, for a particular teacher, and is insufficient in itself to form a true picture of a pupil's 'typical' behaviour. Ideally the pupil should be observed over several lessons, until the observer is satisfied that all aspects of the pupil's behaviour – both positive and negative – have been observed (a skilled Teaching Assistant could be tasked with this).

What should be observed?

Many pupils display more than one type of challenging behaviour. It is not realistic to expect to be able to address and change all behavioural difficulties in one go, so priorities need to be established.

It is vital that the behaviours to be observed are identified and described in observable terms. For example, rather than non-compliant behaviour it would be clearer to describe the number of times the targeted pupil refuses to follow the teacher's instructions/directions.

There are many aspects of a pupil's behaviour that can be studied. For example:

- How does the pupil respond to whole-class or individual instructions?
- Can the pupil work independently?
- How much work does the pupil produce compared with others of the same ability within the class?
- What is the pupil's concentration span?

- Is there a type and duration of restless/inattentive behaviour?
- How much teacher attention does the pupil demand/secure?
- How much time does a pupil spend on or off task/out of his/her seat?
- What is the extent to which the pupil interacts with his/her peers?
- What is the extent to which his/her peers influence the pupil (who specifically?).
- What is the extent to which the pupil disturbs his peers' work?

Carrying out an observation

Once the target behaviour/behaviours have been agreed upon, the next step is to select a method of recording the observations. Using prepared schedules, such as those given as examples within this book, can be useful, although teachers may prefer to design their own. Observations can take a number of different formats.

Narrative observation. This provides a running commentary on how a pupil behaves. It can take the form of a diary that spans a particular length of time, e.g. a day or a week, or it could be single lesson recording that tracks a pupil's behaviour from the beginning through to the end of the lesson. It provides an overview of the range of behaviours – both positive and negative – that the pupil displays.

Time-sampling observation is useful when behaviours are easily identified and occur frequently. It is an effective way of highlighting difficulties that may arise within particular parts of a lesson. However, this type of observation merely records the observable behaviour and can omit influencing factors such as the context in which the behaviour occurs, peer influence, task demands and so on. A useful modification to this type of observation is to select another pupil within the class to observe and act as a control.

Event sampling can give information about the frequency, duration and severity of the targeted behaviour. Recording can be as simple as using a straightforward frequency count, a stopwatch and a rating scale that rates the behaviour from 0 (not evident) to 10 (extreme). Alternatively, this method may be used to record and analyse one particular incident, or infrequent events. Due consideration should be given to the influencing factors such as the context in which the behaviour occurred, events that preceded the incident (**A**ntecedents), the **B**ehaviour itself and the **C**onsequences that have resulted from the incident. This approach is called the ABC analysis of behaviour.

Tracking provides a less in-depth, but longitudinal, picture of how a pupil behaves over a longer period of time, in a variety of contexts with different adults. This is particularly useful for older pupils who are taught by several different members of staff, and can highlight when a pupil has particular difficulties at certain times or in particular curriculum areas.

Incident reporting. In one particular school, all pupils have an individual folder within the ICT system. Any incidents that refer to social and emotional issues and any consequences arising from these, are recorded on the system. If concerns are raised about a pupil by a member of staff, it is possible to track the events and note the interventions that have been made. The 'who, what and where' of incidents can be established and any possible patterns can be determined. Further action can then be put in place.

There is an example of an incident form with appropriate action being taken to resolve the situation in Appendix 4.

This is by no means a fully comprehensive list of all the different types of observation that can be carried out. All of the above formats have advantages and disadvantages. It is important to be aware of observer bias: things should be seen from the pupil's perspective. The only information recorded should be what is actually seen – not the observer's personal inferences. The most important thing is that the approach used works for the observer and results in greater understanding of the difficulties faced by the targeted pupil.

Talk to the pupil

Alongside observations a conversation should be held with the pupil. This could include:

– a discussion about how they feel in a particular lesson;
– what makes them react in a certain way.

Analysing the information gathered

Whatever type of observation is selected, when analysing the resulting information the following considerations must be borne in mind:

- How will the information obtained from the observation be used to plan the ways forward for the pupil's learning and behaviour?
- What are the main causes for concern highlighted by the observation?
- Are the targeted behaviour/behaviours evident in all lessons or are they limited to specific times and places?
- For whom does the behaviour pose a problem – the pupil, the teacher or the pupil's peers?
- Do the highlighted behaviour/behaviours interfere with the pupil's learning or the learning of others? If so, how?
- Does the behaviour put either the pupil or his/her peers/adults at risk? If so, how?
- How do the pupil's peers/adults generally respond to the behaviours causing concern?
- What form will an effective intervention strategy take? How long should this intervention last? How, and by whom, will it be evaluated?

Observations also impart a great deal of information regarding the teaching style and strengths and weakness of the pupil's class/subject teacher; if handled sensitively, this can be a valuable contribution to Continuing Professional Development.

23 Behaviour modification

It is possible that a range of interventions are required both inside and outside the classroom, to modify a pupil's behaviour and maximise his or her learning potential.

The following suggestions may help staff to support a pupil with difficulties.

- Try to understand the pupil and the difficulties they may be trying to overcome. It is essential that relevant background information is shared with staff who work with a pupil having difficulties. The head teacher, SENCo, pastoral team and parents should pass on information (in a confidential manner).
- Discussion should take place with the pupil for them to talk about what is difficult for them and for the teacher to say what the behaviour is that they see as a problem. Only one difficulty should be identified and an improvement should be clarified by both parties, Behaviour modification is most effective when it is done *with* the pupil and not *to* the pupil.
- Targets and a reward system should be put into place.
- Time scales should be set.
- All staff involved with the pupil should be aware of his/her difficulties and reinforce any desired behaviour they observe through positive comments (if this is what has been agreed).
- Attention should be focused on positives; any reward helps the pupil appreciate the efforts they are making. Positive comments and actions help the other pupils see the one with difficulties in a more positive light.
- Parents should be included in any plans and systems could be put in place for them to reinforce appropriate behaviour. Schools may also support parents by rewarding the child for doing the right thing at home, e.g. getting ready for school on time.
- It is important that support is put in for the pupil in difficulty at more unsupported times (breaktimes and lunchtimes), e.g. friendship groups, support to join lunchtime clubs, taking part in a Nurture Group at lunchtime, etc.

- Bear in mind that overnight changes in children's behaviour are not likely: be patient and acknowledge every small success.

The example below illustrates a process of identifying behaviour not conducive to learning; exploring the cause of this behaviour and introducing measures to modify the behaviour.

Questions	Responses
What is the background knowledge about this pupil?	Paul has a supportive family, he appears to be unco-ordinated in his movements
What is the behaviour to be modified?	Paul to start a writing task on request instead of refusing to work
What are the antecedents?	Paul is asked to complete a piece of written work
What are the consequent events?	Paul refuses to work and is doing nothing and irritates his neighbour
Who is present when the behaviour occurs?	Class teacher, class Teaching Assistant
Where and when does the behaviour occur?	In the classroom; whenever writing is expected
Are there particular situations that trigger the behaviour?	An extended piece of work is expected
How intense are the episodes of the behaviour? How long do they last?	Paul is beginning to cause more disruption to his peers… all session
Does there appear to be any sense or meaning to the behaviour?	Paul appears to intensely dislike writing
Talk to the pupil about what they are finding difficult and what they feel they are good at	Paul says he finds it very hard to think of what to say and very hard to write it so that anyone can read it. He says he is good at using computers

A possible intervention: agreed with Paul, his teacher, TA and parents

The teacher will spend a short time recapping what is expected. The Teaching Assistant will support Paul to give some key ideas for his writing and write them on a white board. He agrees to use a laptop to use the notes to write two sentences. He is given a raffle ticket for each sentence he writes and another if he does not disturb his neighbour. When he has gained ten tickets he will be able to play a game on the computer for ten minutes.

Paul's parents agree to read a story to Paul on a regular basis and ask him questions about what they have read. The teacher will support this with relevant reading material and questions. He will also ask the SENCo to do an assessment of Paul's recording skills.

24 Personal Support Plan (PSP)

For those pupils who require a more significant intervention a **Personal Support Plan (PSP)** may be put in place.

The Personal Support Plan (PSP) is a school-based and co-ordinated intervention to help individual pupils to improve their social, emotional and behavioural skills.

A plan is needed for pupils who:

- demonstrate behaviour that is deteriorating rapidly;
- are re-integrating into school following long-term absence;
- are integrating into a new school following a permanent exclusion from their previous school;
- have significant emotional and/or behavioural difficulties following a traumatic life event, e.g. change in family circumstances following separation of parents, a death in the family or being taken into care.

In addition:

- It should identify precise and realistic outcomes for the pupil to work towards.
- It will act as a preventative measure for those at risk of exclusion.
- A nominated staff member should co-ordinate and oversee the PSP planning and process.
- It should be focused on meeting the needs of the child or young person, be practical and manageable. Any PSP should be developed in conjunction with other existing plans and should not be regarded in isolation.
- It may be that professionals consider undertaking a Common Assessment in order to establish how best to support the child or young person.
- Schools should work in partnership with parents and carers so that each understands their roles and responsibilities in relation to the PSP.
- A local authority (LA) representative and/or other relevant agencies may be present to discuss the areas of concern and what is required to get back on track, both academically and socially. LAs may either offer support free of charge to the school, or, if that is its policy, to supplement the school's budget to enable it to buy in the extra support outlined in the PSP.
- The PSP should also specify the agreed support the child or young person and/or the parent/carer needs in order to achieve this.

When running a PSP, bear in mind the following points:

- Be positive about change; look at solutions rather than problems.
- Include the pupil's views by talking to them first and including them in the meeting.
- The potential of the PSP increases where other agencies are involved, and where changes in systems (in school or at home) are made a reality.
- Use the PSP to collate and exchange information, and as a way to look at the whole picture.
- Be clear about boundaries and roles; use subsequent meetings to ensure agreements have been kept, by adults as well as by the pupil.
- Work towards improving outcomes for the pupil as well as for the school.
- View the PSP as a means of inclusion, not a tick-box en route to exclusion.
- Expect that it will not be an instant remedy; give it time to work. Use the PSP to support all participants when there are 'blips'.
- For a pupil with an EHC plan, an interim Annual Review may be required.

There is no set format for recording a PSP and individual schools should develop recording systems that work for them. An effective PSP may include the following:

- pupil details, e.g. name, DOB, gender, year group, family circumstances;
- a pupil's individual strengths/interests – these should include the pupil's interests and achievements both in and out of school;
- details of a pupil's learning style, academic strengths and learning difficulties;
- details and outcomes of previous interventions;
- clear identification of the nature of the pupil's current behavioural difficulties, e.g. frequency, duration, triggers, consequences, impact/reaction of peers/staff;
- details of the planned intervention: targets, provision/resources, staff to be involved, systems of liaising between different parties, how and when the intervention will be evaluated, rewards and sanctions.

Examples of Personal Support Plans

Peter Year 1

In class Peter struggles to remain in his place (particularly at carpet time) and is constantly calling out and disrupting others. At playtimes Peter can be very physical with the other pupils. Many strategies have been put into place but they have been unsuccessful in the classroom. An effective strategy on the playground has been to provide Peter with his own Year 5 playground buddy to play football with and provide him with a good role model.

Pro-active intervention

- Peter has completed six self-esteem sessions with Mrs Richards – Emotional Wellbeing worker;
- referral made to the education psychologist;
- referral made to a paediatrician by Mum.

Effective monitoring

- reward chart to be shared with parents at the end of each week;
- daily verbal report;
- formal review with staff and Mum.

Pupil name: Peter Brown		Class: 1JH	Date of plan: 18.02.16	
SEN stage		SA:	Statement/EHCP:	
Achievement:				
Date of referral to Pupil Referral Unit: Form completed on 22.6.15			Stage of Pupil Referral Unit support:	N/A as yet

Effective rewards:	Effective strategies:	Effective monitoring:
• Verbal praise • Stars/stickers • Reward chart in school – if Peter achieves three positive then another reward is given on the Friday	• Mum informed the school that Peter been diagnosed with ADHD and is now taking 10ml of Methylphenidate Hydrochloride daily • Referral to the sleep clinic made by the doctor • Teacher to repeat clear instructions • Continue to work with Mrs Richards through self-esteem package	• Reward chart to be shared with parents at the end of each week • Daily verbal report to Wellbeing staff • Formal review with senior management staff

Target:
- To sit in his place correctly
- To keep his hands and feet to himself

Effective de-escalation strategies:	Known triggers:	Key behaviours that challenge the adult:
1 Time out away from other children. 2 The use of a buddy (Y6) on the playground. If he refuses or this is ineffective, a verbal warning will be patiently/calmly shared by adult and the expectation that he modifies behaviour in	• Playtimes • New/different teachers • Free times • Being in close proximity to others • Attention • Noises/movement • Any distraction in the class-room	Constant distraction on the carpet Calling out Struggles to sit still

order to get back to Green will also be shared (Peter will move to Amber) If behaviour is not effectively modified, Peter will move to Red and RS will be called.		
Effective sanctions: Amber stage of warning will result in: • minutes off playtime. Red stage of warning will result in: • internal exclusion organised by RS for the next lesson • a telephone call; home/report to Mum at the end of the day – class teacher		**Effective parental support:** • continuing with rewards and sanctions at home • sharing progress in school with parents each week • feedback to school from paediatrician visit

Jon Year 6

In class Jon often exhibits disruptive behaviour, making loud noises (this is particularly noticeable when he is required to work co-operatively with others or listen for extended periods of time). Jon struggles to follow adult instruction and will often lose his temper when he feels that something is unfair. In more unstructured activities Jon is becoming more aggressive towards his peers and extremely oppositional to adults. Many strategies have been tried, including behaviour charts and giving him extra responsibilities but they have been unsuccessful. At crisis point he likes to be a quiet, calm area in order to de-escalate the situation.

At the present time Jon's mum has chosen to take him home for lunch to minimise further incidents. Jon has had a number of fixed-term exclusions

Proactive intervention

• Jon has been provided with a Teaching Assistant for the times he struggles with the most, e.g. PE.
• Jon has completed an anger management package with Mrs Richards – Emotional Wellbeing Officer.

Pupil name: Jon Ellis	Class: 6CE	Date of plan: 01.02.16	
SEN stage	SA:	Statement:	
Achievement:			
Date of referral to Pupil Referral Unit:		Stage of Pupil Referral Unit support:	

Effective rewards:	Effective strategies:	Effective monitoring:
• Verbal praise • Raffle tickets • Team points • Computer time – 10 mins at the end of the day • Drawing/reading comics/ Minecraft (upon completion of work)	• Office job – to take a note/do a job during a 'cool down' period • Sit on his own table for the majority of lessons • Speaking to Jon at all times in a calm manner • Giving Jon a 'quiet area' in PE to retreat to if the noise is too much • Additional TA support in literacy and PE when needed	• Weekly phone call to Mum from class teacher • Daily verbal report • Formal review with staff and Mum

Target:
- Complete set tasks
- Control anger effectively

Effective de-escalation strategies: **Upon displaying challenging behaviour Jon will remain on Green and be offered:** 1 Time out in the area to calm down/ talk to an adult 2 Assistance with his work/or quietly asked to continue with his work, using minimal eye contact **If he refuses or this is ineffective, a verbal warning will be patiently/ calmly shared by adult (Jon will move to Amber)** **If behaviour is not effectively modified, Jon will move to Red and a Senior Leader will be called**	Known triggers: • PE – **strongest trigger** • Being bored/tired • Loud noises • If Jon thinks a decision is unfair • Free reading

Effective sanctions	Key behaviours that challenge:
Amber stage of warning will result in: • Missing the next playtime • Missing some minutes of computer time Red stage of warning will result in: • Internal exclusion organised by RS • A telephone call home • If Jon refuses and will not follow further instructions (ultimately those of senior leaders) which compromises the health and safety of Jon or others – **Exclusion**	• Refusing/not trying • Losing his temper • Stopping others from working
Effective parental support: • Continuing with rewards and sanctions at home • Following Red stage, Mum must attend a meeting in school before Jon returns to the class	

25   Coping with a violent incident

On rare occasions, some pupils lose control and appropriate action needs to be taken.

- Work on the positive, if possible. Look for a way out of the situation, as the child may want one too.
- Ensure that whatever approaches are adopted are carried through.
- Try to defuse a situation and act in such a way as to avoid escalating it.
- Remain calm and in control of yourself. Seek further assistance, if in doubt.
- Ensure the safety of other pupils; it may be appropriate to send them out of the room in the first instance, rather than trying to 'evict' the violent pupil.
- Try to take the initiative by telling the child what you want them to do. Repeat instructions slowly and carefully.
- Practise in your mind what you are going to do before tackling a violent child.

Section 7

Underlying factors

26 Supporting pupils' mental health

Supporting mental health issues

Within schools, one in ten children and young people aged 5 to 16 have a clinically diagnosed mental health disorder and around one in seven have less severe problems.

Schools can mitigate the risk of mental health problems through:

- **providing interventions** for pupils with mental health problems by implementing:
  - a **graduated approach** to inform a clear cycle of support;
  - **assessment** to establish a clear analysis of the pupil's needs;
  - **a plan** to set out how the pupil will be supported;
  - **action** to provide that support;
  - **regular reviews** to assess the effectiveness of the provision and lead to changes where necessary; and
- **recognising that** a wide range of mental health problems might require special provision, including:
  - problems of mood: anxiety or depression;
  - problems of conduct: oppositional problems and more severe conduct problems, including aggression;
  - self-harming;
  - substance abuse;
  - eating disorders;
  - physical symptoms that are medically unexplained.
- **recognising disorders** such as:
  - attention deficit hyperactive disorder (ADHD);
  - attention deficit disorder (ADD);
  - attachment disorder;
  - autism or pervasive developmental disorder;
  - an anxiety disorder;
  - a disruptive disorder;
  - rarely, schizophrenia or bipolar disorder, will also require specialist support.
- **giving support:** pastoral support including access to counselling sessions; specialist provision as required, from local health partners and other organisations.

Only medical professionals should make a formal diagnosis of mental health conditions. Where severe problems occur schools should expect the child to get support elsewhere as well, including from medical professionals working in specialist Child and Adolescent Mental Health Services (CAMHS), voluntary organisations and local GPs.

27 Developing resilience

Resilience is the capacity to bounce back from adversity. Some children exposed to significant risk factors develop into competent, confident and caring adults despite all the odds against them. However, it does not imply that those who are resilient are unharmed by adversity.

> Resilience and adversity are distributed unequally across the population, and are related to broader socio-economic equalities. Those who face the most adversity are least likely to have the resources necessary to build resilience.
>
> (Barnado's, 2014)

There are protective factors that enable children to be resilient when they encounter problems and challenges. There needs to be a counterbalance between social disadvantage, an accumulation of stressful life events and protective features.

> The key factors that promote resilience are 'support from family/and or peers, good educational experiences, a sense of self-belief and opportunities to contribute to family or community life by taking valued social roles.
>
> (Barnardo's, 2014)

The development of resilience aims for effective adjustment in life rather than eliminating all the legacy of childhood difficulties.

As social disadvantage and the number of stressful life events accumulate for children or young people, more factors are needed to act as a counterbalance. The key protective factors, which build resilience to mental health problems, are shown alongside the risk factors in the table.

Support, love and positive relationships are essential for building resilience. Obviously, parents and carers should provide this within the home but this does not always happen to the necessary degree.

Building resilience

Risk factors
- genetic influences;
- low IQ and learning disabilities;
- specific development delay or neuro-diversity;
- communication difficulties;
- difficult temperament;
- physical illness;
- academic failure;
- low self-esteem;
- overt parental conflict;
- family breakdown (including where children are taken into care or adopted);
- inconsistent or unclear discipline;
- hostile or rejecting relationships;
- failure to adapt to a child's changing needs;
- physical, sexual or emotional abuse;
- parental psychiatric illness;
- parental criminality, alcoholism or personality disorder;
- death and loss – including loss of friendship.

Protective factors
- being female (in younger children);
- secure attachment experience;
- good communication skills, sociability;
- being a planner and having a belief in control;
- humour;
- problem-solving skills and a positive attitude;
- experiences of success and achievement;
- faith or spirituality;
- capacity to reflect;
- at least one good parent-child relationship (or one supportive adult);
- affection;
- clear, consistent discipline;
- support for education;
- supportive long-term relationship or the absence of severe discord.

(Resource: 'Building children and young people's resilience in school', Barnado's, 2014)

Schools can help to develop resilience in a variety of ways:

- Having a 'whole-school' approach, which has at its core, a concern for the health and wellbeing of all its pupils, staff, parents and the wider community.
- Early intervention, i.e. in early years or as behavioural changes are observed, is essential.
- Providing breakfast and after-school clubs where pupils are fed and cared for. Homework clubs are important for those whose parents cannot give appropriate support.
- Building strong links with home and school in order to support families, giving parents confidence to support their children appropriately by engaging with school and allowing schools to promote good parenting practices.
- Promoting positive relationships between pupils and all staff within school, which is especially important for those without supportive family relationships.
- Promoting and facilitating supportive friendships between peers.
- Providing structured routines.
- Perception by pupils that all rewards and sanctions are fairly given.
- Positive school experiences where all successes are valued: academic, arts based, sporting, friendship related, community contributions, perseverance.

- Support to develop learning and mastery of skills.
- Strategies to develop self-esteem.
- Encouragement to participate in extra-curricular activities and experiences (financial support may be necessary).
- Opportunities to take part in community projects.
- Supporting transitions from one school provision to another so that these changes do not increase vulnerability and instead resilience is maintained.

For further reading see:

T. Newman (2004) 'What works in building resilience', Barnado's. Available at: www.barnardos.org.uk/resources

'Building children and young people's resilience in schools', Barnado's. Available at: www.barnardos.org.uk

www.actionforchildren.org.uk

---

28 Depression

Feeling low or sad is a normal reaction to stressful or upsetting experiences. When these feelings dominate and interfere with a person's life, it can become an illness.

- Depression affects 2% of children under 12 years old, and 5% of teenagers (Mental Health and Behaviour in Schools, 2016).
- It can significantly affect a child's ability to develop, to learn or to maintain and sustain friendships.
- 10% to 17% of depressed children are also likely to exhibit behaviour problems.

Professional assessment should be considered, if depression is suspected, after a pupil has experienced an upsetting experience.

Prevention/early intervention can focus on:

- Regular work with a small group of children, which could help to change thinking patterns and develop problem-solving skills. These could help to relieve and prevent the symptoms of depression.

If a pupil has been found to have certain problems the following may be considered:

- non-directive supportive counselling for mild depression;
- therapeutic approaches focusing on cognition and behaviour, family therapy or inter-personal therapy lasting for up to three months (in severe cases these interventions are more effective when combined with medication);
- psychoanalytic child psychotherapy for pupils who have depression associated with anxiety;
- family therapy for pupils whose depression is associated with behavioural problems or suicidal thoughts.

29 Conduct disorder

It is thought that 5–7% of all children in the UK are affected by conduct disorder and it is about four times more common in boys than girls.

Causes of conduct disorder

The term 'conduct disorder' applies to children and young people whose behaviour at home or at school is impaired by constant conflict with adults and peers. In adolescents it can go to antisocial extremes and may lead to exclusion from school or trouble with the law. Several factors can interact to result in conduct disorder including individual, genetic, physical and environmental.

Symptoms

Symptoms include:

- fighting and physical cruelty;
- destructiveness;
- lying;
- stealing;
- truancy (including running away from home).

Treatments for conduct disorder

Treatments for conduct disorder include:

- behaviour therapy, including role play, rehearsal and practice;
- psychotherapy, particularly to help with anger management;
- counselling of parents, e.g. helping them to manage at home, medication for depression.

Schools' involvement should include liaising with outside agencies and parents where appropriate.

See the 'Well at School' website.

30 Self-harm

Self-harm is becoming more common. It can take a variety of physical forms: nipping skin, destroying work, cutting, burning, bruising, head banging, scratching, hair-pulling, poisoning and overdosing. It is usually a way for young people to release overwhelming emotions, to trigger pain in order to camouflage mental pain rather than being a cry for attention or an attempt at suicide. Some children may feel they deserve that physical pain. Once they start, it can become a compulsion. It may also be copying behaviour that they have seen in the media or online.

There can be a variety of reasons for self-harm, including:

- loneliness;
- sadness;
- anger;
- numbness;
- lack of control over their lives.

All of these can be linked to depression.

The pupil may be being bullied, under too much pressure to succeed at school, being emotionally abused, grieving or having relationship problems with families or friends.

The physical pain of harming may be less painful than the emotional pain they are feeling and can allow them to feel they have some control over part of their lives. It can also be a way of punishing themselves. Other pupils may notice that their friend has self-harmed or school staff may observe the damage the child has done to themselves.

School staff should note down what they have observed and any comments that a child has disclosed. The Child Protection/Safeguarding person in school should be informed. It may then be necessary to involve the Emergency Safe Guarding and Harm team.

Within school it may be possible to offer diversionary activities, e.g. a stress ball, elastic bands to pick at. The children may also be offered 'drawing and talking' therapeutic art activities, delivered by a trained member of staff.

Refer to the NSPCC website.

31 Eating disorders

For some pupils, particularly teenagers, worries about weight becomes an obsession, which can turn into a serious eating disorder. The most common eating disorders are anorexia nervosa and bulimia nervosa, which are more common in girls, but do also occur in boys. They are evident in young people of all backgrounds and cultures.

Anorexia nervosa: worry all the time about being fat (even if the teenager is skinny) and eating very little; resulting in loss of weight and irregular or non-existent periods.

Bulimia nervosa: worry about weight, alternating between eating little to excessive binges with vomiting or taking laxatives to control weight.

Causes of eating disorders

It is sometimes thought that social pressure from seeing images of ultra-slim models and celebrities can cause or exacerbate eating disorders, but other factors can combine to present a more complex picture:

- family characteristics, e.g. eating disorders, substance abuse or depression;
- personal characteristics, e.g. having an obsessive personality, an anxiety disorder, low self-esteem or being a perfectionist;
- worry or stress leading to comfort eating, which can cause worries about getting fat;
- dieting and missing meals leading to craving for food, loss of control and over-eating;
- a distressing event, such as family breakdown, death or separation in the family, loss of a friend, abuse;
- pressure to be thin caused by a hobby that could become a career, e.g. a dancer.

Symptoms of eating disorders

- significant weight loss or gain;
- saying they have eaten but missing meals;
- persistent preoccupation with food/eating/weight;
- persistent preoccupation with fashion, clothes sizes and/or personal appearance;
- eating alone, in secret or only eating tiny amounts;
- reluctant to eat in public places;
- hidden food or laxatives/diuretics;
- 'grazing' or eating all day or for as long as food is on offer;
- vomiting or regularly visiting the toilet after meals;

- frequently running the taps while in the toilet to cover evidence of vomiting;
- swollen cheeks and/or bad breath from vomiting;
- excessive exercising to burn calories.

Treating eating disorders

Most eating disorder cases will be treated on an outpatient basis. However, in very severe cases an admission to hospital or specialist inpatient centre may be required.

Anorexia nervosa may be treated with:

- psycho-social interventions;
- family intervention to directly address the eating disorder.

Bulimia nervosa may be treated with:

- a course of specially designed cognitive behaviour therapy.

32 Attachment disorder

Babies rely on parents or caregivers to meet their emotional and physical needs and form a bond, or 'attachment' with these adults. Forming this attachment helps children learn to love and trust others, to regulate emotions, become aware of others' feelings and develop healthy relationships in the future. If for some reason this bond isn't formed, children can develop attachment issues – including attachment disorder.

What causes attachment disorder?

Attachment issues come about when a child fails to form an attachment to its parent or caregiver in its early years. The reasons behind this vary, but may include the following:

- no one responds or offers comfort when the baby cries;
- the baby isn't tended to when its hungry or needs changing;
- the baby is abused or mistreated;
- the baby is hospitalised or separated from its parents;
- the baby is repeatedly moved from one caregiver to another;
- the baby receives no attention, so feels alone;
- the baby's parent/s are emotionally unavailable due to illness, mental health problems or substance abuse.

If the attachment disorder is left untreated, it can have a negative impact on the child's emotional, social and behavioural development. A child with attachment disorder may therefore be at higher risk of a number of emotional and mental health problems in later life.

Attachment disorder can lead to:

- behavioural problems: a lack of trust or respect for their teacher, leading to negative behaviour;
- depression or anxiety in social situations;
- learning difficulties;
- low self-esteem and low self-confidence;
- relationship issues;
- substance abuse;
- social difficulties.

Treatment for attachment disorder

Treatment for attachment disorders tends to have two aims. The first is to ensure that the affected child is in a safe environment – a key factor when dealing with cases of abuse and neglect. The second aim is to help the child form a healthy bond with an appropriate caregiver and deal with any residual problems.

Psychological therapy and parenting education is used, including **family therapy, play therapy** or **individual counselling**

See www.counsellingdirectory.org.uk/attachment-disorder.

33 Attention deficit hyperactivity disorder (ADHD)

Attention deficit hyperactivity disorder (ADHD) is a term used to describe a group of behavioural symptoms that include inattentiveness, hyperactivity and impulsiveness.

These characteristics may be noticed at an early age and become more noticeable when children start school: they occur in more than one situation, e.g. at home and school. Most children are diagnosed between the ages of 6 and 12 and can be identified as having ADHD regardless of intellectual ability (but often have learning difficulties): there may also be additional problems, e.g. sleep and anxiety disorders.

Attention deficit disorder (ADD)

Some pupils may have problems with inattentiveness, but not with hyperactivity or impulsiveness. This condition is known as attention deficit disorder (ADD), and it can sometimes go unnoticed because the characteristics may be less obvious.

The main signs of each behavioural problem are detailed below.

Inattentiveness

The main signs of inattentiveness are:

- having a short attention span and being easily distracted;
- making careless mistakes – for example, in schoolwork;
- appearing forgetful or losing things;
- being unable to stick at tasks that are tedious or time consuming;
- appearing to be unable to listen to or carry out instructions;
- constantly changing activity or task;
- having difficulty organising tasks.

Effective teaching strategies

- Implement rewards and sanctions immediately to be most effective.
- Ensure that class rules are clear and simple. They should also be phrased in a positive rather than a negative manner, e.g. 'Please walk' instead of 'Don't run.'
- Reprimand a pupil for misbehaviour privately when necessary, making sure that he/she understands that it is a particular behaviour that is being criticised and not the pupil himself/herself.

- Praise, and positively reinforce desirable behaviour – this can be done either publicly or privately, as appropriate to the individual.
- Seat the pupil near the teacher and surround him/her with positive role models.
- When work has been set, encourage the pupil to verbalise what must be done; first aloud to the teacher or Teaching Assistant, to ascertain that the pupil has correctly understood the instructions, then quietly to him/herself, and finally, silently in his/her head.
- Teach the pupil self-checking strategies aimed at reducing impulsive behaviour, e.g. STAR (Stop, Think, Act, Review).
- Provide immediate and frequent feedback on behaviour and redirection back to task. The pupil should be actively involved in the setting of targets that focus on attention and task completion.
- Seat pupil near positive role models who will not allow themselves to be distracted.
- Accommodate the fact that the pupil may find it easier to work in a quiet area away from the classroom at times.
- Include a variety of activities during each lesson. Introducing a change in activities and position may enable the pupil to return to the original task with renewed focus.
- Seat the pupil at the front of the class and direct frequent questions to him/her to help maintain his/her attention and engagement.
- Work out a non-verbal signal with the pupil, e.g. a gentle pat on the shoulder or a private signal for times when he/she is not attending and when a verbal reminder would be inappropriate.
- Give out work one activity at a time and adapt coursework to the pupil's attention span, breaking longer pieces of work into smaller parts.

Hyperactivity and impulsiveness

The main signs of hyperactivity and impulsiveness are:

- being unable to sit still, even in calm or quiet surroundings;
- constantly fidgeting;
- being unable to concentrate on tasks;
- excessive physical movement;
- excessive talking;
- being unable to wait their turn;
- acting without thinking;
- interrupting conversations;
- blurting out answers before the question is finished;
- little or no sense of danger;
- inappropriate behaviour.

These characteristics can cause significant problems in a child's life, such as under-achievement at school, poor social interaction with other children and adults, and problems with discipline. These pupils will be those who are frequently told off, possibly sit in exclusion areas thinking about how different they are from their peers and generally disliking a school where life is very difficult for them.

Hyperactivity

Some suggestions to support these pupils:

- Acknowledge and discuss the pupil's difficulties with them and involve them in devising strategies that work to support them.
- A pupil with hyperactive or impulsive behaviour will have difficulty sitting still. Instead of always trying to stop excessive movement, include some productive physical movement into lessons, e.g. giving out equipment. Sometimes, simply being allowed to stand at his/her table while completing class work can be effective (as is currently popular with many office workers). Activities need to be carefully managed in order to minimise potential opportunities for misbehaviour.
- Alternate activities that require the pupil to be seated with other activities that allow movement. On some days it will be more difficult for the pupil to sit still than others: be flexible and modify instructional demands accordingly.
- Provide something to 'fiddle with' to overcome constant fidgeting, e.g. Blu-Tack or a stress ball.
- Teach pupils to routinely check their own work before handing it in: this will help them to develop self-checking strategies and to improve rushed or careless work.
- Be alert for early signs of increased restlessness and have diversionary strategies in place, e.g. games, puzzles.
- Activities including colouring complex patterns can encourage concentration (e.g. books such as an inky quest and colouring book, e.g. the Enchanted Forest or the Secret Garden by Johanna Basford, www.laurenceking.com.).
- If the pupil does 'lose control' he/she will need somewhere safe and quiet where they can regain control without been watched by other pupils. Staff should try to keep calm and avoid shouting.

Above all, acknowledge that the pupil is not deliberately misbehaving but in fact has great difficulty sitting still, etc. He may be just as frustrated by the condition as the teacher.

34 Attention-seeking behaviour

Unwanted behaviour in the classroom can be caused by a pupil simply craving the teacher's attention. Such pupils may be observed:

- making excuses – for minor negative behaviour, untidy work, etc.;
- showing a lot of indignation, especially when challenged;
- feigning innocence when held accountable, usually by bursting into tears or by claiming he/she is the one being harassed or bullied;
- constantly trying to be in the spotlight.

Effective teaching strategies

- Within reasonable limits, do not respond to attention-seeking behaviour by giving attention, as this will unintentionally reinforce it. Ignore low-level disruption when possible.
- Deal with the behaviour in as swift and impersonal a manner as possible with minimal speech and eye contact.
- Provide him/her with positive reinforcement (attention) for behaving appropriately. (Catch them being good.)
- Make a point of reinforcing the desirable behaviour of other pupils, e.g. praising those pupils who are lined up in a quiet and orderly manner, rather than chastising the pupil who is causing a disruption.
- Try distraction rather than confrontation.
- Seat the pupil apart from other pupils who are likely to reinforce attention-seeking behaviour, placing him/her near pupils who will ignore poor behaviour.
- Remind pupils of the behaviour you want to see: 'I would like you to wait your turn. When you speak out while someone else is talking, no one can really hear either speaker.'

35 Autism

The term autism is a broad term used to describe pupils with a range of difficulties such as Asperger's syndrome, autism, semantic pragmatic disorder, and pathological demand avoidance syndrome. The term autistic spectrum disorder (ASD) is also commonly used. These difficulties are seen as a continuum and the degree to which pupils are affected will vary significantly.

Autism is biologically based, and can affect pupils across the full cognitive range and may be present alongside other disabilities/difficulties.

There are four key areas of difficulty associated with autism:

- social communication;
- social interaction;
- social imagination; and
- sensory differences.

Pupils with autism may behave inappropriately because of the above rather than being deliberately 'naughty'.

A number of considerations may be necessary in order to develop appropriate behaviour.

- Behaviour and obsessions are often symptoms of anxiety, so look for the underlying cause before reacting to the pupil.
- In order to alleviate some of the anxiety shown by pupils with autism, it may be necessary to change aspects of the classroom/school environment, e.g. changing the seating position of the child in the class to a quieter area.
- Try to provide a consistent daily routine or focus on activities with predictable outcomes: stability is very important for pupils with autism.
- Give examples of how to cope in certain situations. Think about providing a special object to hold when it's their turn to speak/take part.
- Try to structure free choice activities for a pupil with autism. This is often a confusing and frightening experience for them. Try offering a choice of two activities (using objects or pictures to indicate the choices) and gradually introduce more choices over a period of time.
- Always use a calm, clear voice: pupils with autism may become excited and over-stimulated by strong reactions or raised voices.

- Talk to others in the class about the difficulties experienced by pupils with autism. They may not fully understand the extent of their difficulties but it is important, so that they begin to understand the nature of the difficulty.
- Remember that although pupils with autism may appear to listen and understand what is said to them, they may not respond in the correct way. Target the pupil by using their name or touch to focus his/her attention and by repeating group instructions to him/her on an individual basis.
- Try to vary the person who gives the instructions, so that the pupil learns to respond to a range of instructions/pupils/helpers.
- Pupils with autism may have difficulty anticipating the consequences of their actions. Make these clear by writing them down, or showing the consequences using symbols/flow diagrams.
- Use visual cues and clues – visual timetables are particularly effective in helping the pupil cope with what comes next.
- Keep language as simple as possible and be prepared to break down instructions into smaller components. Be specific when using instructions, e.g. 'sit on the blue mat' using a gesture as well, i.e. by patting the mat.
- Use rewards for appropriate responses/behaviour and respond to attempts at communication.
- At times pupils may need to self-regulate by behaviours such as flapping, shouting, rocking – this may occur more when pupil is stressed. Try and teach the child to learn to ask for a break at these times – either by using a symbol, or handing over an object. The pupil then can go to a safe space to regulate themselves.
- Although structures and routines are vital to the wellbeing of a pupil with autism they can also become a problem in themselves. Build some flexibility into daily routines – it can be something simple like a different cup, chair or song. Keep testing the boundaries in a sensitive and controlled way until the pupil learns that changes aren't always confusing and frightening.
- If the pupil begins to establish obsessive routines, then try and intervene before things get out of hand, e.g. warn them that equipment/books will go away in two minutes.
- Provide distraction-free work access, e.g. some pupils may prefer to work at a desk facing a blank wall not situated near a window. Be aware of the environment and try to identify triggers that may provoke undesirable reactions.
- Work on developing independence by choosing tasks/activities that have in-built success.
- Use visual timetables to support the child in understanding the school routine.

Section 8

Continuing Professional Development

36 Planning for Continuing Professional Development

It is vitally important that all staff (including Teaching Assistants, lunchtime supervisors and support staff) understand the school's approach to behaviour management and feel able to deal with challenging situations.

The provision of carefully tailored CPD will help to build colleagues' confidence in this area and develop a consistent approach through the school.

An outline plan of CPD sessions might incorporate objectives such as ensuring that colleagues have:

- a sound knowledge of the underlying causes of behaviour issues;
- an understanding of factors involved in social, emotional and mental health welfare;
- an awareness of various 'trigger points' in different lessons, in the playground, in the dining hall, outside school;
- the confidence to ask experienced colleagues for help and advice;
- a range of strategies to effectively manage whole-class behaviour;
- strategies to address individual needs and reduce barriers to learning.

Format of CPD

The method of delivering professional development will depend on particular factors relating to the school as a whole, and to individual teachers and TAs. The opportunity to learn more about children with behaviour issues will be welcomed by colleagues who recognise children they teach, support or supervise as having difficulties – the issues are then immediately relevant. But it's also important for staff to appreciate that there may be pupils with mental health issues who have not been formally identified.

There are several different formats of CPD to consider:

- **Whole-staff training during a CPD day, or staff meeting.** You may choose to invite an 'expert speaker', a colleague from a neighbouring school (perhaps a specialist school), or a member of your LA pupil support team. If you do choose this option, be sure to brief the speaker adequately. He or she needs to know:

  o the precise range and nature of behaviour issues in your school;
  o what, if any, interventions are in place;
  o details of previous training received by staff.

A school's SENCo is often the best person to plan and deliver such training however, as he or she knows the school, the staff and the children, and can ensure that information and advice offered is relevant and appropriate. Such a person can also build in opportunities for follow-up and on-going development. Be 'in it together'; mutual vulnerability can be a powerful medium for exploring how changes to practice can result in positive developments.

- **Phase, departmental or pastoral group training:** scheduled sessions for particular groups of staff may be focused on learning to use specific approaches or resources.
- **Sharing best practice** (sometimes referred to as 'joint practice development' – JPD): this is more about working together than about transferring knowledge or tips from one educator to another. Activities such as peer observation and shared planning can help to develop a sense of common purpose among staff.
- **Individual mentoring/coaching:** this can be particularly useful where a colleague is teaching a particular student whose behaviour presents significant challenge.
- **Individual study:** colleagues who strive to make good provision for pupils with behaviour issues can become very interested in finding out more, even developing expertise in the field. Pursuing a course of study at university or attending locally provided training should be encouraged and supported – with the proviso that there will be some form of dissemination to colleagues. This course of action can be particularly beneficial to Teaching Assistants tasked with delivering intervention programmes and/or supporting individual children.
- **Encourage professional reading** in small groups or individually. Place new relevant books (including this one!) in the staffroom library; seek out and share articles and research studies as food for thought, as well as reviews of useful resources. Perhaps devote five minutes of meeting time to highlight why you have selected particular reading matter. Encourage staff to contribute to this process too. Perhaps use social networking or your school's virtual learning environment to facilitate it.

An outline for whole-school training on social, emotional and mental wellbeing for pupils

1 Explain the range of social, emotional and mental health difficulties and the different ways that they might impact on behaviour and learning. You might actively involve colleagues in this by giving out a 'sorting activity' of all the various ways that such difficulties can manifest. (Use the grid opposite (Activity 1) and perhaps ask colleagues to prioritise those factors that are the most challenging to identify and/or deal with; or ask them which behaviours they have observed (most frequently) in children they teach.) This is not an exhaustive list – the blank cells can be filled with other behaviours noticed by staff.
2 Ask colleagues if they have ever been in a situation where they could not manage a pupil's behaviour satisfactorily. How did they feel? What could have helped them in that particular situation?
3 What is the school system for referral of pupils with behaviour issues? Is everyone familiar with the process? Could it be improved?

4   Classroom strategies for dealing with low-level disruption: use the lists in this book to help put together a good practice guide.
5   Effective use of Teaching Assistants: is there regular discussion between teachers and Teaching Assistants about behaviour management and how responsibility is shared? Are there guidelines to help shape good practice?
6   Interventions: make sure that staff are familiar with what happens during any mentoring or anger management sessions; can colleagues observe an intervention in action? How can they support and reinforce this work?
7   Parents: how can colleagues garner parents' support and help them to help their children? Use the case studies below (Activity 2) to facilitate discussion (or write an example relevant to your own setting).

Activity 1

Most frequently seen	Most difficult to address	Most difficult to identify	Most serious issues
Talking whilst teacher talks	Getting out of seat	Calling out	Interrupting speakers
Interfering with others' work	Answering back	Crying when told off or criticised	Refusal to co-operate/follow instructions
Pushing etc. in corridor/queue	Failing to listen to teacher/TA	Explosive temper	Physical violence to other pupils
Making too much noise during activities	Cannot concentrate for more than two minutes	Slow to start work/ never completes a task	Constantly fidgets
Quiet, withdrawn; seems disengaged	Over-dominant in group work	Seems to be sad all the time	Does not contribute to discussion or group activity

Activity 2

It can be easy to feel exasperated with parents or carers when their offspring are not behaving in school as you might wish. Consider the case studies below and how you might feel as the parent. What could be done to improve home-school relationships and support the pupil more effectively?

My daughter Kylie is 8 years old and to be fair, she is a little madam. Lippy! She is the eldest of my five kids and does have to help out quite a bit at home. I've got a job in the evenings on three days a week so she looks after them and gives them their tea. She can be bossy, and has sometimes smacked the 5-year-old but they don't come to any harm.

Kylie is always in trouble at school. I'm forever getting letters about her behaviour and I've stopped going to parents' evening because all they go on about is her talking too much and being nasty to the other kids. She started out quite well but now is behind with her reading and writing. The teachers complain that she doesn't do her homework but I don't agree with homework – she has enough to do without that. I was never much good at school myself.

Jason is 13 and to be honest I'm really worried about him. He's always worked hard at school but now his teachers say his grades are dropping. He's always polite and well behaved but his work is not as good as it should be. I've tried to talk to him but he won't discuss things with me – or his dad. He rushes through his homework in about 20 minutes then all he wants to do is play computer games on his Xbox. He doesn't seem to have any friends and spends a lot of time in his room on his own. Our neighbours' boys are always off playing football or something. They look so much healthier than Jason – he's very pale these days, and thin too.

Another letter from the $%&&*! school! As far as I'm concerned, those teachers are clueless about discipline. Our Harry is just full of high spirits that's all. He stands his ground with the other kids and all right, he's been in fights but what teenage kid hasn't? I'm proud of him for standing up for himself. He doesn't like school and I can't blame him. What good did school ever do me? The sooner he can leave the better, though I'm not sure what he'll do then.

37 Evaluating and following up on Continuing Professional Development

Whichever mode of CPD is delivered (you may choose a mixed menu), it's important to evaluate its effectiveness and plan for on-going development. Consider a short evaluation sheet for staff to complete after a training session on behaviour issues, including their suggestions and requests for further development opportunities.

Taking this information into consideration, you can then plan follow-up work to consolidate and build on the training delivered. This provides good accountability evidence for senior managers and OFSTED, and demonstrates the school's (and SENCo's) effectiveness. Ideas for follow-up activities are suggested below:

- a regular 'surgery' where teachers and TAs can seek advice from the SENCo or behaviour specialist;
- optional 'advanced' CPD for interested staff;
- opportunities for teachers to observe intervention programmes – in your own school or elsewhere;
- a working party to trial a new approach, resources or new technology;
- an action-research project to test an intervention and report back to staff on its effectiveness;
- classroom observations by the SENCo to monitor colleagues' effectiveness in providing for the needs of children with behaviour issues;
- detailed tracking of children with behaviour issues to monitor progress and evaluate strategies being used to support them.

References

Barnado's (2014). Building children and young people's resilience in schools. Available at: www.barnardos.org.uk.

Burrell, Andrew and Riley, Jeni (eds.) (2007) *Promoting Children's Well-Being*. Network Continuum, Bloomsbury Publications.

Costell, Bob, Watchel, Joshua and Watchel, Ted (2009). The Restorative Practices Handbook for Teachers, Disciplinarians and Administrators. Institute for Restorative Practices, AbeBooks.

Holland, John and Kingsley, Jessica (2016). Responding to Loss and Bereavement in Schools. Jessica Kingsley.

Newman, T. (2004). 'What works in building resilience'. Barnardo's, available at: www.barnardos.org.uk/resources.

Publications		
Teachers Standards, 2012	Department for Education	www.education.gov.uk/schools
Special Educational Needs and Disability Code of Practice 2014	Department for Education	www.gov.uk
Mental Health and Behaviour in Schools	Department for Education	https://www.gov.uk/government/publications/mental-health-and-behaviour-in-schools–2
Guidance for School Leaders, Staff and Governing Bodies	Department for Education	https://www.gov.uk/government/uploads/system/uploads/attachment_data/file/444051/Use_of_reasonable_force_advice_Reviewed_July_2015.pdf
What works in promoting social and emotional wellbeing ...	National Children's Bureau	www.ncb.org.uk
NSPCC	National Society for the Prevention of Cruelty to Children	www.nspcc.org.uk
One Page Profile	Helen Sanderson Associates (www.helensandersonassociates.co.uk).	
Well at school	Supporting children and young people at school with medical and mental health conditions. www.wellatschool.org	

Appendix 1 Elements of a positive behaviour policy

Common elements of a positive behaviour policy are listed below:

1 Rationale
2 Aims and objectives
3 Rewards and sanctions
4 The role of the class teacher
5 The role of support staff
6 The role of the principal/head teacher
7 The role of parents
8 The role of governors
9 Fixed term and permanent exclusions
10 Screening, searching and confiscating
11 Drug and alcohol related incidents
12 Monitoring and review

Individual schools will enhance and personalise their statutory policy by including the practical day-to-day implementation and evaluation of their policy. This may include a child friendly version of core values, aims etc.

Features of a behaviour policy might include:

Structures and systems: Rules, rewards and sanctions are prominently displayed in every classroom
Rules and expectations: devised by children
Rewards and sanctions: differentiated by age or stage of learning
Lunchtime code
Developing the skills of the children:

- ethos statements;
- SEAL – Social and Emotional Aspects of Learning;
- circle time;
- 'Behaviour for Learning' objectives;
- peer mediators;
- play leaders.

Interventions and multi-agency working:

- Silver SEAL;
- individual behaviour plans;
- pastoral support;

- nurture groups;
- behaviour support;
- Educational Psychology Service (EPS);
- CAMHS.

Developing staff skills:

- staff meetings and training days;
- NQT induction;
- supply teachers;
- training provided by the Local Authority and external providers.

Parents:

- involving parents;
- home-school agreements;
- pastoral team;
- Family Early Help Assessment (FEHA).

Links to other policies:

Ref: http://www.hobmoorschools.co.uk/about-us/policies – Positive behaviour policy

Appendix 2　Example of a behaviour policy

Primary school

Other related academy policies that support this behaviour policy include the Child Protection Policy, Anti-Bullying Policy, Physical Intervention Policy and E-safety Policy and Restorative Practice Policy.

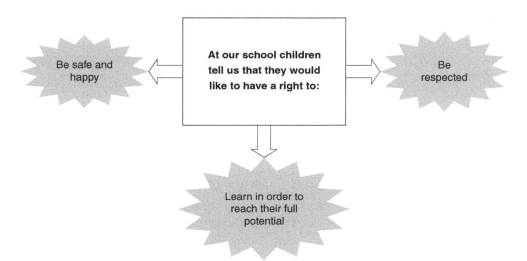

These are our **school aims.** In order to ensure these rights are met, children are expected to develop and uphold the following **responsibilities:**

- Ensure that they keep themselves and others in school safe.
- Participate and maintain a positive attitude towards own learning and that of others.
- Respect themselves, other people and property.

Section 1 – A shared ethos

The school embraces Restorative Practices (RP) as a means of empowering teachers to be successful and effective practitioners within their classroom, raising standards and achievement across the school and developing aspirational, motivated and responsible pupils.

Staff, parents/carers, governors and pupils believe that:

- Most pupils, most of the time are well behaved, work hard and act with care, consideration and politeness.
- Good behaviour and discipline are the responsibility of all stakeholders involved in the school.
- Our pupils need to be taught what our rights and responsibilities mean, and about the behaviour that is associated with them; our pupils will need to be reminded of our codes at appropriate times.
- Praise, positive reinforcement and the raising of self-esteem will all help our pupils develop self-discipline.
- Incidents of inappropriate behaviour should be dealt with restoratively and appropriately. It should be seen as a learning opportunity for the pupil(s) concerned. It needs to be recognised that it is the behaviour we disapprove of, not the pupil(s).

To support this, outstanding behaviour and discipline requires:

- positive relationships between pupils, staff and parents;
- use of Restorative Practice in all aspects of school life;
- clear, fair and consistently applied rules;
- appropriate curriculum so pupils are motivated, engaged and involved in what they are doing.

The responsibilities of staff

In order to ensure that all children are safe, can learn, and be respected, all members of staff have a duty to make sure that the rules that underpin each of these are applied consistently. There should be flexibility shown in the use of rewards and sanctions to take account of individual circumstances. Rules are worded positively to emphasise good behaviour. Where necessary, rules will be discussed with children, especially where health and safety issues need to be understood. Our rules will be displayed in every classroom and on all corridor areas, halls, etc.

Rules for school rules

The children designed the following rules in order to fulfil the three core school aims. They are:

- Be kind to others.
- Act with courtesy and consideration at all times.
- Follow instructions.
- Try my best.
- Use a quiet, polite voice.
- Walk in school.
- Keep our school and its environment clean and tidy.
- Continue to behave responsibly out of school.

In addition, each class develops its own class rules. These are displayed in the classroom and reviewed each term.

Unacceptable behaviour

There is no place for violence, bullying, harassment (racial, sexual or other), vandalism, rudeness, or bad language within our school community. This will never be tolerated.

Staff should be vigilant to signs of bullying or harassment. All such behaviour should be dealt with firmly, in line with the school's anti-bullying policy. Pupils are advised to inform staff whenever bullying or harassment is evident. The 'School Council' should take a leading role regarding information about bullying and prevention.

A clear distinction should be made between minor and more serious misdemeanours, and also between 'nuisance' behaviour and acts that are anti-social, immoral, dangerous or illegal.

When rules are not adhered to

Problems will always occur, however effective our behaviour and discipline policy is. Problems are caused by pupils who forget the rules, by pupils who deliberately flaunt the rules, or by those who are learning and testing the boundaries of acceptable behaviour. In most instances, unacceptable behaviour should be met with surprise and disappointment. Our disapproval should be made clear to the pupil promptly so that they know it will not be tolerated.

In order to maintain a high standard of behaviour and discipline, we need a system of sanctions. These will need to be applied fairly and consistently, take account of all circumstances, including the pupil's age and match the misdemeanours. We should always ensure that we are targeting the right pupil(s). Remember it is the behaviour that is unacceptable, never the child.

Section 2 – Strategies to promote outstanding behaviour

Minor misbehaviour

Minor misdemeanours (throwing pencils, calling out in class) should be dealt with by the adult responsible at the time. Sanctions must, where possible, be immediate and of short duration.

Strategies for minor misbehaviour might include:

- ignoring the pupil – praising the rest of the class – referring to positive behaviour;
- non-verbal checking – eye contact/disapproving frown or shake of head;
- verbal rebuke – reprimand – perhaps lowering of voice – remind pupil of appropriate preventative behaviour;
- keep talking – it could calm anger, but don't talk down to a child who is angry – treat the child with respect and as an individual;
- standing near to the pupil;
- additional work, for example, a letter of apology;
- removal from the scene to another part of the room/area – to work;

- wait outside classroom for five minutes maximum to allow other pupils to settle/ pupil to calm him/herself down.

Pupils may lose their break times if their behaviour or work is unacceptable. Punishments that are humiliating or degrading should not be used.

More serious misdemeanours

For more serious misdemeanours (refusal to follow instructions of senior leaders, serious theft, bullying, harassment, insulting or threatening behaviour, violence, deliberate disruption), further sanctions will be necessary. These may include:

- logging of incidents, where appropriate;
- withdrawing major privilege;
- immediate contact with parents, with attempt to get them to come into school as soon as possible;
- removal from class for longer periods – to another class (by arrangement with other teachers);
- isolation of pupil – this needs to be temporary and justified by the seriousness of the incident and kept under review. It should be used only for the protection of other pupils or staff members, a pupil should never be left alone;
- additional help from outside agencies, e.g. educational psychologists, Pupil Referral Unit.

NB Do not put yourself in a vulnerable position by being alone with a pupil.

Lunchtimes

Our lunchtime staff have the right to expect and receive the same level of good behaviour, including respect and obedience that other adults in school receive from pupils. Where difficulties occur, mid-day supervisors should follow the procedures outlined in this policy statement.

If a child leaves the school premises at the wrong time, please inform the school office immediately.

Section 3 – Procedures

How we monitor and evaluate behaviour over time

Incident reporting

Pupil incident and parental meeting pro formas are made available to all teachers. Incident forms should be completed for:

- all racial (log with Wellbeing Officer) and other discriminatory incidents;
- acts of bullying or harassment;
- serious incidents;
- repeated low-level incidents over a short time frame (especially if this involves the same child/children);

- any other incidents that in the teacher's professional judgement require logging;
- if an individual child has been identified as the perpetrator, regardless of the identity of the victims, the matter should be passed onto the Phase Leader following the third occasion for further investigation.

At lunchtimes, the head teacher/deputy head teacher will be responsible for completing these forms in close liaison with the Senior Lunchtime Supervisor.

All completed forms should be emailed to the deputy head teacher asap, who will be responsible for maintaining a centralised log.

Senior Leaders will regularly analyse the logged incidents to provide some evidence of the range and frequency of the types of incidents that may occur. These outcomes may impact on future provision and identification of specific needs.

How we identify behavioural needs and provide layered support to ensure all rights are met and responsibilities are developed.

An overwhelming majority of pupils	
Description	Teacher has no concerns over behaviour; child can demonstrate ability to follow school rules in and out of the classroom. They may make mistakes occasionally but this is never severe.
Support to develop behaviour over time	<ul><li>Rewards and sanctions</li><li>Gentle reminders</li><li>PSHCE curriculum and SEAL assemblies</li><li>×2 Parents' evenings and annual report</li><li>Agreed class rules</li><li>Responsibilities (jobs, etc.)</li><li>Open door policy to discuss concerns and enhance home/ school partnerships</li><li>Modelling of good behaviour from all stakeholders and outside visitors</li></ul>
Responsibility for monitoring	Class teacher

A very small minority	
Description	Generally behave well but often fail to demonstrate ability to follow school rules at specific times in the school day and/or for all adults. Such instances may be evident either over time or more frequently over a shorter time frame and can be severe.
Support to develop behaviour over time	<ul><li>All support listed above plus:</li><li>Initiate and follow up parent phone call/meetings</li><li>Differentiated rewards and sanctions</li></ul>
Responsibility for monitoring	Class teacher and Phase Leader

Specific individual pupils	
Description	• Frequently lose control, often at specific times in the school day (lessons/lunchtime, etc.). When this happens, severe outcomes may be evident. • Some of the pupils will have an SEND diagnosis but not in all cases.
Support to develop behaviour over time	• All support listed in both sections above plus: • Pastoral Support Programme (PSP) separate to any specific learning plan, which includes the Wellbeing Officer in school being assigned to provide additional support. • At least termly review meetings with parents. • External support from relevant agencies.
Responsibility for monitoring	Inclusion Manager (overseen by head/deputy)

Hot spots – when behaviour incidents are more likely to occur	
Hotspot	*Additional provision*
Transition periods	• Set rules (walk on the left, walk in a line, following teacher's instructions etc.) • Clear Supervision Policy
Lunchtimes (lining up in the hall)	• Supervisor monitors the line • Minimise waiting time
Lunchtimes (playground)	• Activities • Extracurricular clubs • Funded play coordinator • Books to record and monitor behaviour • Playground buddies to support others

Training

The head teacher has the responsibility to identify on-going training needs of staff in respect of necessary skills in dealing with pupils and to make arrangements for such advice/training/support to be available.

Conclusion

This pupil Behaviour and Discipline Policy aims to encourage good behaviour and to develop self-discipline amongst our pupils. The guidelines and range of sanctions, which can be invoked if the need arises, should ensure that all staff are consistent in their expectations. The staff and governors of the school will work in partnership with parents and other agencies, if appropriate, to encourage high standards of conduct, discipline and achievement.

This policy will be monitored and evaluated by governors and staff on an annual basis.

This policy has been written in consultation with all those expected to implement it: teachers, non-teaching staff, Wellbeing workers, lunchtime supervisors, parents, pupils – especially the School Council and governors.

Appendix 3   Example of a behaviour policy

Secondary school

The philosophy

A behaviour policy should promote and protect the rights of all pupils to have equal access to education, including those who have special educational needs that make them vulnerable to behaving inappropriately.

Further, it is essential that the school's policy in relation to the teaching and management of behaviour in school should:

- be publicised to parents/carers, pupils and all staff working in the school;
- have clarity; and
- be maintained.

Governors' duties

As part of its legal duty, and after consulting with the whole-school community, the governing body should compile a statement of principles and aims.

Those that relate directly to behaviour and discipline are as follows:

- to create a safe and secure learning environment in which high standards of behaviour and commitment are clearly expressed and realised;
- to create a culture of high expectations and success for pupils, providing a flexible curriculum that engages and motivates groups of pupils and individuals;
- to promote a sense of responsible citizenship in our pupils;
- to support and facilitate inter-agency work as part of a broader community approach to learning;
- to establish and/or maintain and develop positive working relationships with parents and carers for the benefit of the child;
- to establish collaborative working with other schools.

The whole-school context: a positive behaviour policy

The ethos of the school:

- should be based on the principle of inclusion, which recognises every pupil's right to be included in education;
- is one that accepts and welcomes all pupils; encourages and rewards participation and success; manages, supports and helps overcome barriers to learning.

Teaching and learning

It is every pupil's right to expect excellent teaching and to enjoy learning. The curriculum should:

- offer opportunities that engage, stimulate and challenge;
- be broad, balanced and appropriate for the needs of all pupils;
- promote high standards of learning and behaviour across all subjects from core to periphery, in and beyond the classroom;
- offer different teaching styles that take into account the diversity and choice of pupils' styles of learning.

Procedures and practices should:

- be based on fairness, consistency, self-worth and independence;
- encourage positive attitudes to work and each other;
- show respect for persons;
- be purposefully publicised, demonstrated and taught; provide for a safe, effective and cared-for working environment that promotes excellence and enjoyment and celebrates achievement.

Roles and responsibilities within the school

Head teacher

It is the responsibility of the head teacher to:

- ensure appropriate systems to promote high standards of behaviour and discipline and provide for the effective management of pupils' behaviour, on or off site;
- provide adequate training for all staff in the understanding and discharge of duties;
- to ensure that visiting staff are aware of supporting systems and procedures for the management of behaviour.

Senior staff

It is the responsibility of senior staff to:

- support the head teacher in his/her duties by making sure agreed systems and procedures are made public and implemented;
- to support less experienced or less competent staff in planning for and dealing with problems that might arise.

Teaching staff

It is the responsibility of all teaching staff:

- to support the head teacher in his/her duties;
- to make sure the school's ethos and aims are reflected in their contribution to the life of the school;

- to contribute to the joint planning of an appropriate curriculum that supports pupils' learning whatever barriers there might be;
- when planning their own lessons to give consideration to the development of supporting strategies that promote desired behaviours and manage undesirable behaviours;
- to set realistic social and behavioural targets for pupils;
- to consult with other staff on issues related to individual behaviour management issues;
- to apply relevant training in relation to the management of behaviour;
- to follow school protocols and guidelines when dealing with pupils;
- manage behaviour effectively to ensure a good and safe learning environment;
- to share concerns with senior staff as a means of preventing predictable problems.

Support staff

It is the responsibility of all support staff:

- to support the head teacher in his/her duties;
- to make sure the school's ethos and aims are reflected in their contribution to the life of the school;
- to contribute to the joint planning of an appropriate curriculum that supports pupils' learning whatever barriers there might be;
- to support the teaching staff by following agreed systems and procedures;
- to follow school protocols and guidelines when dealing with pupils;
- to apply relevant training in relation to the management of behaviour;
- to share concerns with teaching/senior staff as a means of preventing predictable problems.

A whole-school approach to managing behaviour triggered by social and emotional difficulties

- A school should be proactive in supporting all pupils in order to promote good behaviour and to prevent undesirable behaviour occurring rather than just managing it.
- However, it is acknowledged that a child experiencing social and emotional difficulty will require a plan to be put into place.
- A whole-school focus is the most effective way of minimising or preventing the occurrence of behaviour problems.
- Whole-school policies should unite staff towards a common ethos in which all staff feel supported when faced with children displaying challenging behaviour.
- The head teacher, Senior Leadership Team and Governing Body must lead on a positive school ethos that is reflected within the school's policies and procedures. The policies and procedures must have an emphasis on promoting positive behaviour and embedded strategies to support pupils with their social and emotional difficulties.
- Curriculum content and how it is delivered are important influences on pupils' behaviour.

- A small minority of incidents may require the pupil to be physically managed by staff. Schools should have a physical intervention policy and all staff should be very clear about the procedures involved.
- A whole-school behaviour policy and ethos is key.
- Pupils with social and emotional difficulties need to have their needs addressed within the school organisation. This requires planning and flexibility with good communication between staff, parents and the pupils. There needs to be a clearly identified outcome that all parties are working towards achieving. The journey to the outcome is populated with well planned and implemented milestone objectives.

Appendix 4   Guidance policy for enhancing community relationships and learning for a school with Restorative Practice (behaviour policy)

Relationships and learning at our primary school

At our primary school we believe that every member of our school community should have an equal opportunity to achieve his or her full potential regardless of race, colour, gender, disability, special educational needs or socio economic background.
We believe that it is the right of all our pupils to be educated in an environment free from disruption by others.

This policy sets out the framework for the behaviour, responsibilities, values and attitudes expected of our community members within a Restorative Practices philosophy.

Restorative Practices aims to build the community and to repair and strengthen relationships within this community.

The school embraces Restorative Practices (RP) as a means of empowering teachers to:

- be successful and effective practitioners within their classroom, raising standards and achievement across the school and developing aspirational, motivated and responsible pupils;
- create a consistently orderly environment, both inside and outside of the classroom, which will enable everyone to work and learn;
- reward students for academic achievement, completing and returning homework, being equipped for school and behaving well in lessons;
- ensure that Every Child Matters agenda is firmly embedded into all aspects of school;
- embed the use of Restorative Practices in all aspects of school life.

Restorative Practices philosophy statement

Effective Restorative Practices foster awareness of how others have been affected by inappropriate behaviour. This is done by actively engaging participants in a process that separates the deed from the doer and rejects the act not the actor, allowing participators to make amends for the harm caused.

Restorative Practices acknowledges the intrinsic worth of the person and their potential contribution to the school community.

A Restorative Practices framework will:

- Improve behaviour and attitudes.
- Provide explicit tools within a defined framework to challenge unacceptable behaviour, resolve conflict and repair harm.
- Improve relationships; establish rights, accountabilities and responsibilities to the community.
- Provide a safe, philosophical basis for staff, pupils and parents to share ideas and discuss issues.

There are four key elements of Restorative Practices. These are:

- social discipline window;
- fair process;
- restorative questions;
- free expression of emotions.

Wherever possible we should try to offer high support, nurturing and encouragement in conjunction with consistently setting clear boundaries and expectations of behaviour. Staff should always, within their professional conduct, be positive and respectful role models to their pupils.

At our primary school we believe it is best to do things *with people*. Wherever possible you should use fair process and our responses to challenging behaviour should involve building relationships and repairing harm. It is our aim that our community follows this Restorative Practices framework.

An Introduction to Restorative Practice for parents/carers

The aim of Restorative Practice (RP) is to develop community and to manage conflict and tensions by repairing harm and building relationships. This is our priority as a restorative school, as we see ourselves at the heart of and serving our community. Restorative Practices:

- Allow the act (unacceptable behaviour) to be rejected, whilst acknowledging the intrinsic worth of the person and their potential contribution to society.
- Separate the 'Deed from the Doer'.

It is a process that puts repairing harm done to relationships and people over and above assigning blame and dispensing punishment. It shifts the emphasis from managing behaviour to focusing on building, nurturing and repairing relationships and deciding on possible consequences for chosen actions.

It has been proven that a whole-school restorative approach can contribute to:

1   A happier and safer school
2   Mutually respectful relationships
3   More effective teaching and learning
4   Reduced exclusions
5   Raised attendance

116

6   Addresses bullying behaviour
7   Raises morale and self-esteem
8   Helps promote a culture of inclusion and belonging
9   Increases emotional literacy

As part of the RP process, children and staff will be involved in meetings and restorative circles that include:

The five RP questions

1   What happened?
2   What were you thinking about at the time?
3   What have your thoughts been since?
4   Who else has been affected by what you did?
5   What do you think needs to happen to make it better?

If your child has been harmed emotionally or physically by the actions of others a restorative circle will be held using the following questions:

1   What did you think when you realised what had happened?
2   What have your thoughts been since?
3   How has this affected you and others?
4   What has been the hardest thing for you?
5   What do you think needs to happen to make things better?

Restorative Practice is *not* just about questions. It is about a process that is seen as fair: allowing free expression of emotions and significantly is about offering high levels of support, whilst challenging inappropriate behaviour through high levels of control, encouraging acceptance of responsibility and the setting of clear boundaries.

All school staff, teaching and non-teaching have had (as a minimum) basic training about Restorative Practices whilst many have also attended enhanced training to try and ensure that our intentions translate into actions.

All of our pupils understand and use restorative circles in their everyday school life. As part of our commitment to RP, you as a parent/carer may also on occasions be asked to contribute to a restorative meeting if this is felt to be the right course of action.

It is important that staff deal with situations to establish and develop their own relationships. Aim to separate the deed from the doer and the act from the actor as integral to Restorative Practice philosophy.

Children are encouraged to challenge each other's behaviour. We begin by telling the children to hold up their hand and use the phrase 'STOP! I don't like it when you do that, it makes me feel...' Initially, we spend a lot of time thinking about emotions so that children can express how they feel effectively, e.g. '.....it makes me feel sad, angry, upset, hurt, worried, anxious, etc.'

We find this is a very visible way of allowing children to feel confident about stopping something they don't like.

With thanks to Collingwood Primary School, Hull

Appendix 5   A sample pupil incident form

Pupil name: Richard		Class: 5DB		Date: 12.1.16	
Staff present: Mrs Delaney			Other pupils present: Paul		
Time: (please tick)		Location: (please tick)		Incident type: (please tick at least one)	
Arrival		Main hall		Absconding	
AM registration		Classroom		Disruption	
Lesson 1		Playground		Ignoring adult direction	
Break		Gym		Physical aggression towards an adult	
Lesson 2		Toilets		Physical aggression towards a pupil	
Lunch (eating)		Corridor		Verbal abuse towards an adult	
Lunch (activities)		Changing rooms		Verbal abuse towards a pupil	
Lunch (lining up)		Other classroom, e.g. ICT		Not completing work	
PM registration		In transition		Damage to property	
Lesson 3					
Break					
Lesson 4					
Departure					
Other (please specify)		Other (Please specify)		Other (Please specify)	

Details of incident (please detail any triggers if known and any de-escalation techniques used and what you did at the time)
During a play fighting game at lunchtime Paul accidently caught Richard's side. Richard said it really hurt him, so he punched Paul in the nose.
Details of outcome/way forward
Restorative circle held. Both boys agreed on what had happened. They also agreed that they shouldn't have been play fighting and that they wouldn't play fight in the future. They apologised to each other. They decided that as a consequence Paul should miss 5 minutes of his playtime and Richard should miss 15 minutes. RS telephoned both set of parents who were extremely supportive and said that they would speak to the boys that evening. We checked in on both Richard and Paul the next day and they informed us that they are now friends and there have been no further problems.
Report compiled by: R. Francis **Date: 12.1.16**

Appendix 6 One school's staged framework to manage behaviour

Cause of concern	Monitoring	IBP	Continued IBP	PSP	Post PSP
Inappropriate behaviours picked up through termly monitoring of SIMMS behaviour record	Added to behaviour register monitored weekly by Assistant Headteacher	Moved up a stage on behaviour register monitored weekly by Assistant Headteacher	Continued on same stage, Assistant Headteacher to monitor. Advice sought at SMT review meeting	No improvements to behaviour and may receive fixed term exclusions. Demonstrates serious behaviours that place in danger of exclusion	To remain in school is no longer appropriate
Support menu	Support menu	Support menu	Support menu	Support menu	Support menu
Positive class environment Rewards and sanctions as in school policy Celebration assemblies Gold stickers Praise pads Golden Time Playtime buddies Lunchtime clubs Responsibilities, e.g. KS 1 lunchtime, monitor Class SEAL/PSHE Investors in pupils; personal targets Class charters Catch being good; give positive reinforcement Quality first teaching Language of choice	Weekly monitoring by Assistant Headteacher Specific rewards Parents aware of concerns Weekly phone call home Updated home/school agreement Solution focused conversations	IBP with specific targets for pupils and strategies for staff Personalised reward system Parents aware of concerns Weekly phone call home Nurture room outreach support Other Nurture room programmes considered – PALS, PEARLs, P and P, art therapy, positive futures, sport leadership Enhanced TA vigilance Active listening sessions Social, emotional and behavioural competencies profiles – updated regularly	IBP with specific targets for pupils and strategies for staff Personalised reward system Parents aware of concerns Weekly phone call home Nurture room outreach support (individual) – 'Draw and Talk', 'Time to Talk' considered Behaviour Support Service – telephone advice	PSP with specific targets and strategies Personalised reward system Personalised behaviour log 1 to 1 support Meeting with parents SEN consultant Educational psychologist Behaviour Support Service referral Reduced timetable Curriculum alternatives provided Boxall profile Risk assessment of behaviours completed External mentor Chance UK	Managed move Permanent exclusion SEN statement identifies mainstream not appropriate

SEAL involves the emotional aspect of learning for those lacking social connections.

Positive futures is for pupils who may struggle with transition to the secondary school and is based on sports leadership with younger pupils and is led by external groups.

PALS – Positive Active Lifestyles is for selected pupils with activities that include exercise and cooking good food.

P and P – Peter and Paul, the caretakers, will give pupils who need time away from the classroom, opportunities to carry outdoor activities (as part of a structured programme).

The following strategies can be applied at any point during the above framework:

Nurture room outreach support
Lunchtime clubs
Scales and goals
Tokens, stamps
Use of SEN consultant
Pupil premium – mentor support if appropriate
PSA support
Intensive restorative circles
Social stories
CAF
EWO
Traffic lights
Time out cards
Home/school book
Visual timetables
Access to ICT and other specialist equipment
Doodle bug books
Modelling
Tangle
Consider diet influence
Relaxation
Visualisation

Appendix 7   Primary pupils

Examples of rewards and sanctions

If a pupil has an individual good behaviour card or equivalent, it is important that a discussion has been held with the pupil to arrive at a mutual decision about the specific behaviour being rewarded.

+ = + = + = + Punched cards + = + = + = +

The pupil is given a special good behaviour card. At the end of the activity/day, the pupil's card is punched, to reward good behaviour. If the pupil achieves a previously agreed total, he/she receives an appropriate reward.

= + = + = + Pulling sticks + = + = + = +

Pupils earn up to five lolly sticks in one lesson. These are displayed on the pupil's desk. If the pupil receives all five sticks by the end of the lesson he/she is rewarded appropriately.

+ = + = + = + Hanging paper-clips + = + = + = +

Pupils earn paperclips for good behaviour in order to make a chain of 20. An agreed reward is then given.

+ = + = + = + Jumping frogs + = + = + = +

Good class behaviour helps the frog to jump to a lily pad. If the pupil makes it to the end pad by a previously agreed time, a reward is given.

+ = + = + = + 1-2-3-4-5 + = + = + = +

When the pupil behaves well, a number is written on a laminated card that is placed on the pupil's desk. If the pupil continues to behave well and achieves 1-2-3-4-5 by the end of the lesson, he/she is rewarded appropriately.

+ = + = + = + Behaviour agreements/contracts + = + = + = +

Displayed in the classroom, these can act as a visual prompt and help to remind the pupil that his/her behaviour is the pupil's choice.

+ = + = + = + Connect 4 + = + = + = +

Drop counters down. Get four in a line and the class gains a reward.

+ = + = + = + Golden time + = + = + = +

This is given when the class, cumulatively, gains points, and golden time is given at the end of the week. The activities, which are given as rewards, can be decided by the children making suggestions and the favourite for the week being voted upon. Activities could be making and eating toast, making plasticine models and so on.

This can also be a whole-school approach, in that all children can gain points that allow them to have access to golden time at the end of the week.

+ = + = + = + Stars on the board + = + = + = +

Given for pupils who are observed to be behaving well, e.g. working on task or listening to the teacher. If the class earns sufficient stars then pupils have a few minutes' extra playtime.

+ = + = + = + Table rewards + = + = + = +

Given for the group of children at a particular table who have tidied their table well after a craft session or worked quietly during the session. They have a small treat determined by the teacher.

+ = + = + = + Golden table at lunchtime + = + = + = +

For pupils who have been chosen for good behaviour; being kind, trying hard, listening to a story.

+ = + = + = + **Star tubs** + = + = + = +
These are placed on a table and have a star put in as the teacher observes good working practice. The table with the most stars by a certain time gains a reward.

+ = + = + = + **Attendance cup** + = + = + = +
The class with the best attendance of the week gains the cup and a 15-minute treat.

+ = + = + = + **Modelling good behaviour** + = + = + = +
This is a way to remind some pupils of what they should be doing and to praise others for appropriate behaviour. Comments such as 'Oh, look, John and Emily are picking up the cubes' may encourage more tidying up; 'Paul has written two lines already' may spur others to more writing.

+ = + = + = + **Over-the-top comments** + = + = + = +
Making positive comments, which appear slightly 'over the top' but give pupils a boost. 'How did you do this; it's so good?'; 'How are you always getting so many ticks on your work?'

+ = + = + = + **Star of the day** + = + = + = +
A particular pupil's photograph is displayed in a 'frame' with a comment underneath stating why he/she is a star. The credit could be given for good work, being especially kind to a classmate or listening well. The whole class could make suggestions or the teacher could make the choice.

+ = + = + = + **Helper of the day** + = + = + = +
The pupil could have his/her photograph placed on the wall.

+ = + = + = + **Helping with school pets** + = + = + = +
Could be a reward.

+ = + = + = + Earning a treat + = + = + = +

Identify what the pupil enjoys through observation or by asking him/her what he/she likes doing. The pupil has to earn points through a jointly agreed scheme for achieving an appropriate behaviour, e.g. putting up his/her hand, not shouting out, remaining in his/her seat. The points could be recorded on a chart, and if the agreed amount is collected the pupil receives a 'treat'. It may be necessary to 'treat' often in the initial period and slowly build up the time that the pupil has to achieve the desired behaviour.

+ = + = + = + Quick notes + = + = + = +

A small certificate could be given by the class teacher on an *ad hoc* or regular basis for any behaviour that represents an achievement for a particular child.

+ = + = + = + Courtesy cards + = + = + = +

Given by members of staff to pupils who are observed being polite and well behaved when moving around school.

+ = + = + = + Good news phone calls + = + = + = +

Made to parents about their child (sometimes parents hear only negative news about their children).

+ = + = + = + Head teacher's award + = + = + =

A special sticker or certificate given by the head teacher for an achievement by a child.

+ = + = + = + Certificate assembly + = + = + = +

Letters are sent home to parents to invite them to a special assembly where certificates to commend good behaviour are given out. The parents and children are then invited to have drinks and biscuits after the assembly.

+ = + = + = + Star of the week + = + = + =

Chosen from the whole-school, or one from each class. The pupils' photograph is displayed on a noticeboard and a report about him/her appears in the weekly school newspaper.

+ = + = + = + Reward cards + = + = + = +

Varying types: apple trees, ladybirds, dinosaurs with outlines for spots to be put on, when the pupil carries out the required, agreed behaviour.

+ = + = + = + Balancing scales + = + = + = +

Use a set of balancing scales and some colourful weights. One side of the scale represents good/positive behaviour, and the other side represents less than desirable behaviour. Pupils attempt to keep the scale in balance or weighted to the positive side. Weights may be added to reinforce specific incidents, or whenever a lesson or activity is completed.

+ = + = + = + Traffic-light cards + = + = + = +

The pupil will need a red, yellow and green card. These should be pinned on the classroom wall. If a pupil behaves inappropriately he/she is asked to pull the green card off the wall, leaving the yellow card exposed. If the yellow card must be pulled off, leaving the red card exposed, the pupil receives a previously agreed sanction, e.g. five minutes of time out. If the red card must be pulled off, the pupil gets a slightly more severe sanction, e.g. ten minutes of time out. If at the end of a lesson the pupil has retained his/her green card a suitable reward is given.

+ = + = + = + Card system – 3 colours + = + = + = +

Top card = green; two crosses = yellow; two more crosses = red; two more = no card. The pupil can earn any number of good behaviour points on yellow and green. If a pupil earns five behaviour points out of a possible seven, he/she has the choice of a reward or to fast-track to green the next day.